Power in Presence

A Guide to Effective Business Conversations

Power In Series

Effective communication is a reflection of your professional identity. If you want to set yourself apart as a leader and open doors to new opportunities, you need to hone your ability to communicate so you influence, persuade and inspire.

Already available

Power in Precision: A Guide to Effective Business Writing

Effective writing is crucial for career success. It's your voice in the world and the vehicle for your influence. *Power in Precision* offers practical strategies to refine your writing, express your ideas more clearly and elevate your career.

Forthcoming publications in the *Power In* Series

Power in Perception: A Guide to Effective Data Visualization

Power in Perception shows how to create clear and persuasive data visualizations that transform complex data into actionable insights, resulting in thoughtful decisions and better outcomes.

Power in Persuasion: A Guide to Effective Presentation

Power in Persuasion teaches professionals how to turn ideas into powerful, persuasive messages in the form of compelling presentations, stories and speeches that will resonate with myriad audiences.

You can access additional *Power In* series content by scanning the QR code or by visiting our website (www.powerinseries.com).

Power in Presence

A Guide to Effective Business Conversations

Mark Watson

Inform. Persuade. Inspire.

Power in Presence: A Guide to Effective Business Conversations

Self-Published by: Portcullis Consulting, LLC, Concord, MA

Copyright © 2025 by Mark Watson. All rights reserved.

Published in the United States of America.

First Edition

Editor: Francesca Forrest

Cover Design: Darcy Kelly-Laviolette

Inside Design: Mark Watson

No part of this publication may be reproduced, stored in a retrieval system, or transmitted in any form or by any means—electronic, mechanical, photocopying, recording, or otherwise—without the prior written permission of the author, except as permitted by the United States Copyright Act of 1976. Requests for permission should be addressed to admin@portcullisconsulting.com.

LIMIT OF LIABILITY/DISCLAIMER OF WARRANTY: The author makes no representations or warranties with respect to the accuracy or completeness of the contents of this work and specifically disclaims all warranties, including, without limitation, warranties of fitness for a particular purpose. The advice and strategies contained herein may not be suitable for every situation. The author shall not be liable for any damages arising from the use of this work.

For more information about *Power in Presence*, visit www.powerinseries.com.

Publisher's Cataloging-in-Publication Data

Names: Watson, Mark, 1969-, author.

Title: Power in presence : a guide to effective business conversations / Mark Watson.

Series: Power In Series

Description: Includes index. | First edition. | Concord, MA: Mark Watson, 2025.

Identifiers: LCCN: 2024927595 | 979-8-9913615-5-2 (hardcover) | 979-8-9913615-4-5 (paperback) | 979-8-9913615-3-8 (ebook)

Subjects: LCSH Business communications. | Communication in management. | Interpersonal communication. | BISAC BUSINESS & ECONOMICS / Business Communication / General | BUSINESS & ECONOMICS / Business Etiquette | BUSINESS & ECONOMICS / Careers / Career Advancement & Professional Development | BUSINESS & ECONOMICS / Leadership

Classification: LCC HF5718 .W38 2025 | DDC 658.4/5--dc23

Table of Contents

Introduction: Elevate Your Professional Conversations Through Presence — 1

Part 1: Foundations of Effective Conversations — 3

Appreciate the roles of conversations in business — 5
- Know the various types of business conversations — 5
- Know how to converse your way to stronger business relationships — 6

Use conversations to share knowledge, collaborate and make decisions — 7

Be genuine and authentic — 7

Know how to tell your backstory — 9

Know your personality type, but don't be hostage to it — 10
- Work on developing coping mechanisms — 10
- Be proud of being "atypical" — 11

Part 2: Meeting Management — 13

Learn the common types of meetings — 15

Know how to get and schedule meetings — 15
- Know how to request a one-on-one meeting — 15
- Interact with executive assistants respectfully — 16
- When convening meetings with multiple attendees, respect others' calendars — 17
- Remember workdays have boundaries — 17
- Thank those who schedule your meetings — 18

Know how to prepare for meetings — 19
- Prepare for a meeting, but don't overprepare — 19
- Research who you are meeting — 19
- Think carefully about what pre-read or meeting materials to require — 20
  - Limit materials for smaller meetings or forego them — 20
  - Only send pre-read materials when they will significantly improve a meeting — 21
- Help junior colleagues prep for success; don't just throw them in — 21
  - Listen to your junior colleague practice and offer constructive feedback — 21
  - Offer additional support, feedback and congratulations — 22

Know how to start and run a meeting 22

Be on time 23
Invest time in introductions 23
When the meeting merits it, use the Chatham House Rule to promote candor 24
If you took time to prepare an agenda, lay it out first before diving in 24
Maintain the right altitude in the discussion 26
Know how to manage question-and-answer segments 26

Know how to manage interpersonal dynamics in meetings 27

Stay focused on being the chair, not a participant 27
Don't let someone commandeer the meeting 28
Know how to balance speaking time so meetings are inclusive 28
Get comfortable interrupting 29
Handle interruptions gracefully 30
Use silence to elicit engagement; it really is golden 30
Have some prepared or planted questions 31

Know how to conclude a meeting 31

Drive towards the decisions and outcomes you desire 31
If you put "next steps" on the agenda, get to next steps 32
Use mind maps to recap a meeting 32
End a meeting on time 33

Be prepared for the unique challenges of virtual meetings 34

Know how to follow up on meetings 35

Part 3: Advanced Conversational Techniques — 37

Master nonverbal dynamics 39

Dress appropriately 39
Know how to introduce yourself and what you do 40
Be confident, even when you aren't 40
Straighten your posture 41
Spell and say people's names correctly 42
Address people by name when you're talking to them 42
Show interest in people and remember personal details that matter to them 43
Maintain eye contact 43
Read body language and mood in the room 44
Offer, don't seek, credit 46

    Lighten the mood with humor.. 47

Use questioning and active listening for deeper engagement 48
    Just ask the question—don't preface it with "I have a question"................................... 48
    Ask questions that open up the dialogue.. 48
    Engage others in the discussion early on 50
    Practice active listening... 51
    Create space for real-time and reflective thinkers... 52
    Let people tell their go-to story, even if you've heard it before.................................... 52
    Know how to revive a dying conversation 53
    Know how to take notes effectively and unobtrusively... 54

Choose language that's easy to understand 54
    Use simple words and limit or eliminate overused or specialized language 54
    Avoid overstating or overqualifying your remarks 56
    Learn the lingo, but don't use it excessively 56
    Be conscious of using filler sounds like "um" and "uh"... 57

Make your conversation memorable through stories and comparisons 57
    Become an effective storyteller... 57
        An example of storytelling: misselling and the green cabbage.............................. 58
    Make data relatable in conversations.. 59

Build trust through self-awareness and balanced dialogue 59
    Know when to use "we" instead of "I"... 60
    Be mindful of accentuating hierarchy 60
    Avoid dominating the discussion 61
    Be careful clarifying someone else's comments in public... 61

Handle conflict with confidence and clarity...62
    Stay off politics and religion in conversations.. 62
    Don't ignore major problems... 63
    In a leadership role, aim for impartiality when managing conflict 64
    If there's complete misalignment, walk backwards until there isn't............................ 65
    Be prepared to agree to disagree, just not all the time 66

Part 4: Fine-Tuning Your Conversation   67

Stay informed to contribute meaningfully to discussions 69
    Keep current on news and business 69
    Keep abreast of the topics that constitute office small talk... 70

Broaden your horizons—and bring that knowledge into conversations 70
- Learn from work interactions 71
- Step boldly out of your comfort zone 71

Communicate inclusively, respecting cultural differences 72
- Be mindful of your idioms and metaphors 72
- Use gender-neutral and nonableist language 72

Handle conversational danger zones with care and professionalism 73
- Think before complimenting someone's appearance 73
- Use swear words sparingly, if at all 74
- Manage and limit your interactions with sharp-elbowed colleagues 75

Part 5: Feedback and Career Conversations — 77

Deliver constructive feedback with empathy and clarity 79
- Only offer feedback if you are in a legitimate position to do so 79
- Use "the effect on me" technique 80
- Distinguish impact from intent in feedback conversations 80
- If asked, offer imprtial career feedback 81

Actively seek feedback for continuous improvement 82
- Ask for real-time feedback for ongoing improvement 82
- Embrace 360-feedback for your overall career arc 83

Use conversations to manage your career trajectory and celebrate accomplishments 84
- Take charge of your career through self-advocacy 84
- Be proud of yourself and encourage others to congratulate themselves 85

Consciously choose your work-life balance 86
- Be deliberate in you work-life decisions 86
  - My personal wake-up call 87

Conclusion: Cultivate the Art of Being Present — 89

Exercises for Sharper Conversations — 93

Index — 111

Introduction: Elevate Your Professional Conversations Through Presence

Your skill in conversations can set you apart as a leader and communicator, whether you're leading a team meeting, pitching an idea to a senior executive or handling a difficult discussion. Your attentiveness, your ability to hear what's being said and to add your own ideas in the right way and at the right point—in a word, your presence—can make all the difference.

Being present in conversations means more than just showing up physically; it's about being fully engaged, aware and attuned to the dynamics of the moment. Your focus, body language and tone all contribute to how your message is received and how others perceive you. In an era of constant distractions, the ability to be fully present is a powerful advantage. It builds trust, creates stronger professional relationships and influences outcomes.

Mastering the art of conversation is about knowing when to listen, when to speak and how to adapt your approach based on the situation. A master of conversation fosters an environment in which everyone feels heard and valued, leading to a more positive work environment and ultimately to more positive outcomes.

Power in Presence is designed to guide you through the nuances of effective business conversations. It outlines the foundations of effective communication and offers tips to master advanced techniques. You will learn to manage challenging interactions with confidence and develop the skills to communicate in a way that resonates with diverse audiences, all while showing up as your genuine self. Each section of the book is packed with practical strategies that will equip you to handle any conversational scenario with clarity and poise.

As you progress through *Power in Presence*, remember that the goal is to improve your ability to converse and truly connect with others. By being present, listening actively and speaking with intention, you can transform your conversations into powerful tools that inform, persuade and inspire.

The book is structured as follows:

- **Part 1: Foundations of Conversations:** This section lays the groundwork for successful business interactions by exploring the core elements of effective communication: authenticity and presence. It emphasizes the importance of showing up as your true self, understanding your communication style and harnessing your strengths. The focus is on building relationships through genuine dialogue, setting the stage for more meaningful conversations.

- **Part 2: Meeting Management:** This part offers a comprehensive guide to preparing, leading and following up on meetings to maximize productive outcomes. It includes practical strategies for organizing agendas, managing time effectively and creating an inclusive environment where everyone's voice is heard. By mastering these skills, you'll transform meetings from routine obligations into powerful forums that drive collaboration and decision making.

- **Part 3: Advanced Conversational Techniques:** Delving deeper into the art of communication, this section covers the nuances of body language, questioning techniques, active listening and storytelling, as well as how to build trust by being self-aware and how to deal with conflict. It provides insights into how to read the room, engage others with empathy and tell compelling stories that resonate. These advanced skills will refine your ability to transform everyday interactions into engaging, productive conversations that offer opportunities for influence and connection.

- **Part 4: Fine-Turning Your Communication:** This part focuses on activities that will further hone your communication skills, such as keeping up with the news and being aware of topics of interest to your colleagues, as well as guidance on inclusive language and sensitivity to cultural differences regarding personal remarks and swearing, all of which are important in today's interconnected and multicultural workplace.

- **Part 5: Feedback and Career Conversations:** The final section is dedicated to mastering the delicate art of giving and receiving feedback, guiding career discussions and advocating for your professional growth. It offers practical tips on building credibility when offering feedback, engaging in constructive career conversations and taking charge of your professional development. This part emphasizes creating a culture of continuous improvement and self-advocacy, empowering you and your colleagues to reach your full potential.

Let this book be your guide to mastering the art of presence in business conversations. By committing to full engagement and authenticity, you will unlock new levels of influence and inspire those around you to reach their highest potential. *Power in Presence* offers more than just new skills—it promotes a mindset that can transform the way you lead, connect and succeed in your career.

PART 1

Foundations of Effective Conversations

Part 1 introduces conversations as the cornerstone of success in business relationships and notes that authenticity and self-awareness are central to successful conversations.

In Part 1

- Appreciate the role of conversations in business.
- Use conversations to share knowledge, collaborate and make decisions.
- Be genuine and authentic.
- Know how to tell your backstory.
- Know your personality profile, but don't be a hostage to it.

Appreciate the roles of conversations in business

Conversations are the foundation of success in any business. They are where relationships are built, ideas are exchanged and decisions are made. Conversations go beyond mere information sharing; they provide opportunities to connect, align and create understanding. Appreciating their variety and the roles different types of conversation play is the first step in becoming skilled at them.

Know the various types of business conversations

Conversations in business come in many forms: some are formal while others are casual; some have a narrow focus while others are more wide ranging. Recognizing the different types is a prerequisite for adopting an approach that fits the situation. Knowing how to handle each type is the mark of an effective communicator, one who builds strong relationships and collaborates in clear decisions that result in productive outcomes.

- **Informal conversations:** These are the spontaneous chats that happen in hallways, during coffee breaks or at casual team gatherings. Informal conversations are crucial in building rapport, creating a sense of camaraderie and strengthening professional relationships. The key is to be approachable, be present and genuinely show interest in the people with whom you interact.

- **Formal meetings:** Meetings are formalized conversations: those present at a meeting make presentations, ask questions and engage in exchanges over the topics that occasioned the meeting. During meetings, strategies are developed and business decisions are made. Unlike informal conversations, meetings typically are aiming for a particular outcome and require preparation. At the most basic, there are two types of meeting:
    - **Small group discussions:** These are intimate, focused conversations that typically involve two to five participants. They provide an opportunity to focus on specific issues or goals in depth and can be used for detailed brainstorming or personalized feedback. Because they have fewer participants, small group discussions allow for more candid exchanges than are typical in larger gatherings. It is important to keep these conversations productive, inclusive and targeted toward the desired outcomes.
    - **Larger group meetings:** These involve a broader audience, often including multiple departments or stakeholders, and usually have a higher degree of formality. They require a structured agenda, clear roles and a focus on maintaining engagement across the group. If you are the convener of a larger meeting, it is important to encourage participation

from all attendees. As with smaller meetings, large-group meetings should not lose track of their purpose and objectives.

- **Remote and virtual conversations:** We have over a century of experience with one form of remote conversation in business—namely, telephone conversations. Virtual meetings via video technology, which experienced exponential growth during the COVID-19 pandemic and afterward, are newer, but have become thoroughly embedded in business life. These types of conversation pose distinct challenges because they lack many of the in-person cues we rely on in conversation, such as body language and, in the case of telephone (or video, if the camera is off), facial expressions. To participate in and manage these discussions effectively, you must adapt your communication style, use the technology to your advantage and promote active engagement.
- **Feedback conversations:** Feedback enables personal and professional growth, but delivering and receiving it effectively takes practice. Feedback conversations require tact, empathy and honesty to be constructive. When done well, these interactions build trust, encourage development and motivate the feedback receiver to improve. If you are receiving feedback, being present means listening actively and taking to heart what the feedback giver is attempting to communicate. If you are giving feedback, being present means keeping in mind the receiver's perspective and delivering your message in a way that's respectful and direct.
- **Career and performance discussions:** These conversations focus on career growth, setting expectations, evaluating performance or discussing future opportunities. The key to these conversations is to approach them with clarity about your own objectives while being open to feedback and realistic about the opportunities for advancement.

Know how to converse your way to stronger relationships

Strong relationships are built through meaningful, consistent conversations. Whether with clients or colleagues, these interactions form the basis of long-lasting professional connections. It's not just—or even mainly—about speaking: listening and striving to understand the entire message behind what's being said is equally important. We all want to share our own ideas, but you should also aim to listen and demonstrate that you value others' perspectives:

- **Show genuine interest in others:** Ask thoughtful questions and truly listen to responses. People appreciate it when someone remembers small details from previous conversations and checks in on them later. It shows you value the relationship beyond surface-level interactions. When you are present and listening, you pick up on these details and are able to respond in a way that builds deeper connections.
- **Communicate clearly and respectfully:** Use simple, concise language that avoids jargon. This shows respect for others' time and intelligence. Be direct without being abrupt, balancing brevity with a friendly tone. When you're present and paying attention to others' reactions, you'll be aware of when the conversation needs more clarity and when lighten the mood to keep things comfortable.
- **Tailor your style to the person:** Not everyone communicates the same way. Pay attention to others' communication styles and adjust yours accordingly. This might mean taking a more formal tone with some, while using a relaxed, conversational approach with others. Attention to the person you're talking to helps you pick up on these cues and adjust your approach in real time.
- **Follow up to keep relationships alive:** After an important conversation, it's never amiss to follow up with a quick note or a brief conversation. This helps solidify the connection and shows that you're invested in maintaining the relationship. Presence in conversations helps you recognize the key moments that deserve follow-up, so relationships don't fizzle out after a single exchange.

> "Choose to focus your time, energy and conversation around people who inspire you, support you and help you to grow you into your happiest, strongest, wisest self."
>
> — Karen Salmansohn, behavioral change expert and author

Use conversations to share knowledge, collaborate and make decisions

Understanding how conversations are used in spreading knowledge, working together and making decisions will help you improve how you approach dialogue for all three purposes.

- **Share knowledge without overwhelming:** When sharing insights or expertise, focus on what's most relevant. For example, if you're sharing findings of a new survey, focus on the major themes or changes over time using the most striking data, rather than getting sidetracked with every survey finding under each theme. Break complex ideas into digestible pieces and make space for others to ask questions, offer feedback or share related insights. Being present allows you to gauge when you've shared enough or when more clarification is needed.

- **Encourage open collaboration:** For collaboration to work, everyone needs to feel comfortable contributing. Let others voice their ideas and actively listen (for example, by reflecting back your understanding of what you're hearing). Demonstrate your engagement during these conversations by giving speakers your full attention. When people see that you're truly listening, they feel more inclined to collaborate.

- **Drive conversations toward outcomes:** Business meetings can easily meander if there's no clear objective. Keep the conversation focused on outcomes by regularly checking in with questions like, "What are the key takeaways here?" or "What decisions need to be made today?" Presence is key here—staying focused on the goals of the meeting so discussions don't drift aimlessly.

- **When making decisions, balance assertiveness with flexibility:** Conversations involving decisions often require a delicate balance. If everyone in the room has equal power regarding the decision, be assertive expressing your opinion but understand that others may come with the same degree of commitment to a different solution. Of necessity, you must be flexible regarding the outcome. People will be more likely to collaborate with you if they see you are open to different perspectives.

> "Good communication is as stimulating as black coffee, and just as hard to sleep after."
>
> — Anne Morrow Lindbergh, aviator and writer

Be genuine and authentic

Authenticity is at the heart of effective communication. Being yourself in conversations builds trust, fosters genuine connections and encourages open dialogue. When you show up as your true self, without masks or pretenses, you invite others to do the same. This truth is well recognized: business books, leadership workshops and executive MBA courses preach the importance of being genuine and provide tools and strategies to make it happen. The irony is that the minute you start using an overly prescribed method to display your authenticity, you're no longer being authentic. It's a performance, and eventually people see through it. Worse, maintaining that act is exhausting, and it can create more stress than it's worth.

> "Authenticity is a collection of choices that we have to make every day. It's about the choice to show up and be real. The choice to be honest. The choice to let our true selves be seen."
>
> — Brené Brown, philosopher and public speaker

Authenticity is about showing up as the real you—in your personal life and in the workplace. It's not about performing yourself as a role, much less pretending to be something you're not or putting on a mask that you think fits a corporate mold. Keep the following in mind for interacting naturally as the person you really are:

- **Be yourself even when it's not easy:** It's easy to be yourself when you meet no resistance, but being authentic means staying true to who you are, even when you encounter pressure to change. Take a simple, common work example: small talk about sports. If you're not interested in sports, don't feel obliged to fake enthusiasm just to fit in with a conversation at the office. If the group has energy in discussing sports, it's fine to be more of a listener, especially if seeking to change the topic to one you favor may halt the discussion too abruptly. However, if there's room to redirect, it's okay to say, "Actually, I'm not really into sports, but did I hear you like camping, too? I'd love to hear about spots around here that are good for camping." Or, if you don't know much about the person, you can volunteer a topic that you're interested in: "How do you feel about movies? Have you seen any good ones recently?" This makes it possible to create a more genuine connection, saves you from faking an interest for years to come and teaches by example a way of negotiating a shift in topic.

- **Be authentic regardless of the people you're interacting with:** You shouldn't just turn on authenticity when it's convenient or when you think it will make you look good. Being genuine means bringing the same level of honesty and openness to all interactions, whether you're talking to a junior team member, a client or your boss. Naturally, you'll adapt your behavior based on who you're speaking to, but true authenticity means you don't change your core self to suit different audiences.

- **Be willing to admit to mistakes:** Authenticity is not about perfection—no one is perfect. You may feel afraid to admit your mistakes, but they are part of you too. True authenticity includes admitting when you're wrong, being open about areas where you have room to improve and acknowledging your strengths and weaknesses. When you're willing to say, "I don't know the answer to that" or "I made a mistake," you show that you're only human, which builds trust and fosters a culture of honesty. It can be a powerful way to connect with others on a deeper level.

> "To dialogue, it is necessary to know how to lower the defenses, open the doors of the house, and offer human warmth."
>
> — Pope Francis

- **Speak your truth without fear:** Authenticity means not routinely applying a filter to your thoughts just because you're worried about how they'll be received. Too often, we hold back from speaking up because we're afraid of rocking the boat or being seen as a troublemaker. But being authentic means trusting your own insights enough to voice them, even when they might challenge the status quo. You don't need to shake things up recklessly; thoughtful and constructive honesty can make all the difference. Sometimes the workplace becomes stagnant because everyone's too afraid to stir the waters. For example, if you're going to be working with colleagues who always work weekends, but you don't and you don't expect your team to either, you can ask if the work can be structured and sequenced so it's possible to complete it within the work week. The question may create some initial friction, but often norms continue simply because no one has suggested alternatives, or if they did ask, they didn't do so with conviction. A little ripple can prompt new ideas and lead to progress that wouldn't have happened otherwise. (See "Don't ignore major problems" in Part 3 for more on this topic.)

- **Remember that the authentic you grows and changes:** Just as everyone makes mistakes, everyone grows and changes. Authenticity doesn't mean adopting one posture and sticking with it forever. Your thinking and attitudes will evolve as you learn more and as circumstances change—and you should be open to this process. The key is that change and evolution should come naturally, not because you're being pressured to conform to someone else's idea of what you should be. As you progress in your career, remain grounded in your core values, but don't be afraid to adapt to take on new challenges.

> "Always be yourself, express yourself, have faith in yourself, do not go out and look for a successful personality and duplicate it."
>
> — Bruce Lee, martial artist and actor

Know how to tell your backstory

Part of being yourself in professional settings is knowing how to tell your backstory in a way that's engaging, concise and relevant. Your backstory is much more than a list of your jobs or accomplishments—it's the narrative that connects your experiences, values and career trajectory into a cohesive story that draws in those who hear it. Here are some points to remember when telling it:

- **Identify the main contours of your career:** Your story should highlight key turning points in your career or life. These turning points—a major career shift, for example, or a major challenge you overcame—offer insight into how you've grown and what motivates you. Think about the key moments that shaped you and be ready to tell them in a way that feels natural.

- **Avoid the temptation to embroider:** It's tempting to embellish or tailor certain parts of your backstory to fit what you think others want to hear, but what really happened is what made you who you are. Good storytelling doesn't require altering the facts: how you tell the story will showcase your unique voice and reflect your personality and values. The more you tell your story, the more confident you will feel about your narrative.

- **Adjust what aspects of your backstory you share to align with the situation:** If you're in a casual networking setting, you can keep it more personal, focusing on why you entered your industry or what excites you about your work. In more formal settings, such as a workshop or client meeting, emphasize your role or professional achievements in the context of the current conversation or opportunity.

- **Be informative, but concise:** A well-told backstory should be concise—around two or three minutes at most—and avoid too much detail. The goal is to give enough information for others to understand where you're coming from, but not overwhelm them with your entire life history.

Know your personality profile, but don't be a hostage to it

Personality assessments like the Myers-Briggs Type Indicator (MBTI), TRACOM and others offer fascinating insights into how people think, behave and interact with the world. Who doesn't enjoy discovering their personality type—whether you're an INTJ, an ESFP or somewhere in between on the MBTI scale—and seeing how your traits align or contrast with those of others?[1] Understanding your colleagues' profiles can enhance teamwork by revealing potential sources of friction or where collaboration might thrive. This awareness helps you anticipate challenges and better use each other's strengths.

However, while these assessments can be useful, you mustn't let them box you—or anyone else—in. It's one thing to say, "I'm a natural introvert," but quite another to use that label as an excuse to avoid activities that push you out of your comfort zone.

At their best, personality profiles offer a broad framework for better understanding yourself. Perhaps you're a strong introvert (scoring high on Introversion in the MBTI) who finds solace in solo work, or you might be someone who thrives on spontaneity (scoring high on perception) and resists structured planning. These insights can validate your tendencies and highlight your natural strengths. But relying too heavily on a personality profile can create mental barriers and lead you to feel restricted, as if certain behaviors are off-limits because they don't align with your type.

Work on developing coping strategies

Understanding your natural tendencies is just the starting point. The real value lies in using that awareness to adapt, grow and succeed even in environments that may not perfectly align with your preferences. If you are willing to step outside your comfort zone, you will discover opportunities to broaden yourself in unexpected ways.

For instance, if a strong introvert is left to their own devices, they may prefer to work in isolation most of the time. But professional success often requires visibility, collaboration and occasionally taking the lead in social situations. To address this, introverts can develop strategies to manage their energy levels and shift their behavior based on the moment's needs, blending their natural inclinations with the demands of their role. For example, as an Introvert on the MBTI scale, I know that if I'm leading or actively participating in multiday workshops or trainings, afterwards, I need to schedule days free from too many group meeting to recharge emotionally and physically. If I don't, my energy levels dwindle further, and I can become irritable or unfocused. Likewise, someone who is an Extrovert, in MBTI terms, has to learn how to stay focused and energized when working alone.

Understanding your personality profile can help you work more effectively with others because you are aware in advance of when your preferences may not suit a situation and can plan ways to adjust. For example, someone with a strong preference for spontaneity and flexibility may thrive in creative environments but have difficulties in settings that demand strict deadlines and precision. Someone who has this self-knowledge can choose to collaborate with colleagues who excel at structure and organization, using their strengths to create a sense of accountability and

---

[1] The MBTI categorizes personality using four scales of what are described as opposite characteristics: extraversion (E) and introversion (I) for sending and receiving energy, sensing (S) and intuition (N) for gleaning information, thinking (T) and feeling (F) for decision making and judging (J) and perceiving (P) for approaching the outside world. The combination of people's preferences on each of the four scales forms 16 distinct personality types, such as INTJ or ESFP, that offer insight into one's natural tendencies.

focus. Working alongside more structured teammates can help you develop disciplined habits, even if they don't come naturally. Similarly, if you know you're detail-oriented but struggle with big-picture thinking, partnering with vision-oriented colleagues can help broaden your perspective. It can also help the big-picture thinker better appreciate the need for detail and fact-based opinions. The goal is to find strategies that use your strengths and those of the people around you to enhance your collective effectiveness.

Be proud of being "atypical"

Being atypical isn't a disadvantage—it's an asset. When everyone else is walking a conventional path, being the one who took a detour allows you to see opportunities and solutions others might miss. Instead of trying to blend in or forcing yourself onto the paths of others, embrace what makes you different. By pushing the team to consider alternative viewpoints, you will be preventing the kind of groupthink that often stifles innovation and creativity. That's where your true value lies and that's what will set you apart in your career. People recognize that the strength and fortitude it takes to forge your own path are essential qualities for leadership and success in any field.

Moreover, what's considered typical is constantly evolving. What's standard today may be outdated tomorrow. Industries shift, trends change and the skills or qualities that seem atypical now may become the most sought-after traits.

Be vigilant, however, when labels implying atypicality are used. These labels can carry negative connotations, and their use may reveal biases, especially when they intersect with gender, race or background. For example, being called "opinionated" might sound neutral at first, but assess whether it's meant to highlight that you're known for having strong, informed views—or if it's code for being difficult or argumentative. If it's being used in this way, it can be damaging and may be the result of a hidden bias.

If you or your colleagues are labeled in ways that seem unfairly negative, particularly when those labels are applied more harshly based on gender, race or other factors, don't hesitate to push back. Language matters, and so do the labels we accept. If someone refers to you as "intense" or "assertive," ask yourself: is this feedback consistent across the board? If you are a woman or a person of color, consider whether a male or white colleague would be described the same way for similar behavior. If not, it's important to challenge these stereotypes politely but firmly. Clarify your position and stand up for yourself and your colleagues when labels feel unjust.

> "I love interesting people with eccentric stories and outsiders of the world."
> — Paloma Faith, singer-songwriter and actor

* * * * *

Understanding the foundations of conversations is the first step in building stronger relationships and collaborating effectively. By being genuine, sharing your story and embracing your unique qualities, you set the stage for meaningful interactions in any business setting. Now, let's turn our attention to managing meetings—a vital aspect of professional life where effective preparation, respect for others' time and thoughtful leadership can make all the difference in achieving your desired outcomes.

PART 2

Meeting Management

Part 2 focuses on mastering the art of meeting management, beginning with a survey of the types of meetings you are likely to encounter. The guidance that follows applies mainly to one-on-one, small and medium-sized meetings, though some can be adapted for larger meetings and conferences.

In Part 2

- Learn the common types of meetings.
- Know how to get and schedule meetings.
- Know how to prepare for meetings.
- Know how to start and run a meeting.
- Know how to manage interpersonal dynamics in meetings.
- Know how to conclude a meeting.
- Know how to follow up on meetings.

Learn the common types of meetings

Meetings generally fall into five categories, each with different characteristics:[2]

- **One-on-ones:** These can be informal (e.g., a quick catch-up) or formal (e.g., a performance review or a meeting with a senior client).
- **Small meetings (3–10 people):** These can be informal (e.g., team updates), semiformal (e.g., project reviews) or formal (e.g., client presentations).
- **Medium-sized meetings (10–20 people):** These tend to be semiformal (e.g., larger project updates, trend discussions) or formal (e.g., workshops, committee meetings or professional networking events).
- **Large meetings (20–50 people):** These are generally formal, often bringing together stakeholders for industry initiatives or broad organizational updates.
- **Forums and conferences (50+ attendees):** Typically formal gatherings, these involve industry professionals or members of a profession and are focused on knowledge sharing and networking at scale.

Know how to get and schedule meetings

There is more to securing and scheduling meetings than just sending out calendar invites—the process is about navigating professional relationships with tact and consideration. Successfully getting a meeting requires understanding the value of others' time, workday boundaries, location and time zones. If you are interacting with executive assistants (EAs), getting a meeting means understanding and appreciating their role and developing a rapport with them.

Know how to request a one-on-one meeting

Getting on someone's calendar can be a challenge, especially when dealing with busy executives or influential people. If you're already known to the person and past conversations have been valuable, you're in a much better position. First, determine whether they manage their own calendar or have an EA who handles their schedule. If they manage their calendar themselves, reach out directly in a call or via email. Be clear and concise about the purpose of the meeting and suggest a time frame, but remain flexible to accommodate their schedule. If they have an EA, it's best to copy them in

---

[2] The strategies set out in this section will enable you to lead or contribute to formal committee discussions, but the guidance does not cover specialized committee management tasks like conducting votes or taking official minutes.

your initial outreach and then follow up with the EA, or, if you have a closer relationship with the EA, simply email the EA directly.

If it's a cold outreach, you'll need a compelling hook and a connection:

- **Craft the hook:** This is your "why"—the reason this person should give you time. The hook must be from the recipient's perspective, not yours. What will they gain from meeting with you? Are you offering to share valuable insights about industry trends, discuss a new report or present a new product or service? Think about why they should care about the topic and why having this conversation with you specifically is worth their time. Be specific about the benefits they will derive from the meeting.

- **Establish a connection:** In a cold outreach, having a shared connection or common ground often increases your chances of getting a meeting:
    - **Highlight a referral:** This is the best connection. For example, "Kathryn, Charlotte Gravell suggested I reach out to you" provides instant credibility since you're being referred by someone they trust.
    - **Cite a common acquaintance or affiliation:** A common acquaintance or affiliation (such as a board or organization) is slightly less powerful than a referral, but still strong. For instance, "I see you're on the board of SAW Corp. You must know Charlotte Gravell; she and I go way back to college" creates a sense of familiarity and shared connections.
    - **Note a common educational or business background:** This option should be used carefully. "I see we both attended Richmond" or "I noticed we were both at McKinsey together" are examples that can work. Only mention the commonality if you were likely to have overlapped in years or had a strong shared experience. Otherwise, it can feel generic and impersonal, akin to saying, "I see we both grew up in Boston."

    Avoid creating artificial connections. I knew one executive who wanted to meet a senior leader to whom he had no connection. After learning that the executive was a golfer, he followed him around a charity event, took photos and later sent a framed photo as a way to request a meeting. While it worked in that case, it's a risky move that could easily backfire because it can be seen as overly intrusive or disingenuous, potentially damaging your reputation.

- **Leave a voicemail outlining your follow-up strategy:** If your initial outreach is by phone, be sure to have a well-prepared script. If you get through to voicemail, be clear about who you are, why you're reaching out and what the next steps are. You might say, "I'll follow up with an email" or "I'll reach out to your EA to get on your calendar." This approach keeps the process in your control, rather than leaving you waiting for a call back that may never come.

Interact with executive assistants respectfully

Good EAs are fiercely protective of their executive's time, and for good reason. Time is one of the most valuable resources executives have, and it's the EA's job to see that their time is used effectively. Many business books refer to EAs as gatekeepers—a term that often carries a negative connotation, implying their primary role is to block access. In reality, EAs are not there to push you away; they're there to evaluate whether what you're asking for is a good use of their executive's time. EAs can be extremely helpful if approached respectfully and thoughtfully:

- **Make initial contact:** When you reach out to an EA, be clear about who you are (especially if you don't have an established relationship with the EA) and, more importantly, why the meeting would benefit their executive (not what you hope to gain). This makes it easier for the EA to assess whether your request aligns with the executive's known priorities and interests.

- **Respect the process:** Recognize that the EA isn't going to interrupt the executive's day just to ask if they'd like to meet you. Ask politely that they mention your request when next they review the calendar with the executive. This approach respects the EA's role and leaves the decision-making process in their hands. It demonstrates patience and an understanding of how the executive's time is managed.

- **Think twice about bypassing the EA:** Some business gurus encourage you to "go around the gatekeeper," but this is a highly risky tactic. It's one thing to send an email to an executive and mention that you'll follow up with their EA—it's entirely different if you deliberately bypass the EA because they've blocked you before or you assume they will do so now. Taking this route can damage your reputation. EAs have long memories, and they won't appreciate you undermining their role.
- **Say thank you:** Always thank the EA for their help, whether you get the meeting or not. Acknowledging their assistance goes a long way toward building a respectful relationship and can make future interactions smoother and more collaborative.

When convening meetings with multiple attendees, respect others' calendars

Respecting other people's calendars is part of professional courtesy. When scheduling meetings, don't simply pick a time that works for you and expect everyone else to rearrange their day to accommodate your meeting. This is inconsiderate, inefficient and signals a lack of respect for other people's time and priorities. When you're the one organizing the meeting, any conflicts that arise are your problem, not theirs, so adopt the following procedure:

- **Review everyone's calendar using available tools:** Most of us use shared calendars, like Google Calendar or Outlook, which makes it possible to see others' availability. Before scheduling a meeting, take a few minutes to review the calendars of those you're inviting. Look for any conflicts and avoid double-booking people. If their schedule shows them as busy or unavailable, don't simply assume they can move things around for you. Instead, reach out to them to see when they might be free. If it's difficult to find a time that works for everyone, consider offering more potential time slots or using a tool like a Doodle poll so invitees can choose the options that works best for them.
- **Pay attention to out-of-office markers:** Most calendar tools offer important clues on people's availability. For example, in Outlook, when a time block is marked in purple, it means the person is out of the office, which, as the name suggests, means they're not available. It doesn't matter if they're on vacation, attending an off-site or dealing with a personal commitment: if you see an out-of-office marker, assume they're not going to attend your meeting. They may not even see your invitation in time if you chose to ignore their lack of availability and send one.
- **Be mindful of time zones and distance:** For virtual meetings or calls, don't assume everyone is working on the same clock as you. Especially if you are working with colleagues or clients in different regions, keep in mind that meeting that works perfectly for your afternoon could fall into their very early morning or late evening, which could be frustrating for them. And especially if you're scheduling in-person meetings, keep in mind where people are coming from. Is this early-morning meeting going to require a participant to take a predawn flight in order to attend?

Remember workdays have boundaries

In today's hybrid and always-on work environment, the lines between professional and personal time can easily blur. Don't contribute to this problem. Scheduling meetings or calls that push into your team's personal time suggests you consider their well-being to be secondary to immediate business needs.

Instead, respect reasonable workday and weekend boundaries to promote a productive and healthy work-life balance for your colleagues and yourself:

- **Avoid early-morning or late-night calls:** We've all gotten calendar invites for a late-evening or early-morning call, and most of us feel obligated to accept. But before you send such an invite, consider what that time means to others. Your invitees may have kids to get to school, dinner plans with family or just need that hour for themselves to recharge before or after a long day. Constantly infringing on these personal hours chips away at the personal time that's essential for everyone's well-being.

- **Avoid late calls on Fridays:** Calls scheduled after 5:00 p.m. on a Friday are equally inconsiderate. Is the topic really so urgent that it can't wait until Monday? If you're scheduling a late call on Friday to impress a colleague or client with your dedication, consider that they have probably already gone home for the weekend and won't even see your message or materials until Monday anyway.

- **Weekends should be off-limits when it comes to work:** Respecting weekends shows you value your colleagues' well-being and want a sustainable pace that keeps everyone healthy and motivated. People need time to recharge, and burning out your team for short-term gains is a surefire way to lose their commitment and loyalty in the long run.

Effective planning can typically eliminate the need for weekend work. If a deadline falls on a Monday, aim to have everything wrapped up by Friday. Create realistic timelines that allow your team to meet objectives without last-minute scrambles. If weekend work is truly unavoidable, be transparent about why it's necessary and acknowledge the extra effort your team is putting in. Above all, don't protect your own weekends while expecting your team to sacrifice theirs. There's nothing more demoralizing than a leader who routinely insists on keeping their time off intact while piling last-minute tasks on the team. If you wouldn't willingly give up your own weekend for a project, presentation or proposal, don't expect your team to do so either.

Thank those who schedule your meetings

Let's be honest: coordinating meetings, managing schedules and dealing with endless back-and-forth emails to find availability is one of the most tedious aspects of the workday. It's exasperating and time-consuming, which is why, if you are fortunate enough to have an EA to handle these tasks, you should let them know how much you appreciate their work.

Good EAs are invaluable. They handle the behind-the-scenes logistics that keep you organized and efficient. Get to know them personally—don't treat your interactions as mere transactions. Ask about their family, their interests and what matters most to them. A bit of personal interest goes a long way in nurturing a positive working relationship and a sense of mutual respect.

Just as they protect your calendar, respect theirs. When you know they're out of the office (and they'll usually let you know), avoid emailing or calling them expecting immediate responses. Instead, acknowledge their personal time and handle urgent matters yourself or wait until they return. When you do connect, don't always start with what you need; take a moment to ask how their weekend was or how they enjoyed their recent vacation. Genuine interest in their well-being helps to build a stronger, more collaborative relationship.

Taking a moment to thank them might seem like a small gesture, but it means a lot to the recipient. Recognition shouldn't be reserved for one day of the year; it should be part of your daily routine. A simple thank you or acknowledgment of their effort shows that everything they do to keep everything running smoothly doesn't go unnoticed.

Know how to prepare for meetings

Effective preparation helps keep meetings productive and focused. Depending on the nature and purpose of the meeting, preparation may include conducting targeted research, creating relevant materials or prepping your colleagues. Whatever the particulars, thoughtful preparation sets the tone for meaningful discussions and successful outcomes.

"You should never go to a meeting or make a telephone call without a clear idea of what you are trying to achieve."

— Steve Jobs, entrepreneur and cofounder of Apple

Prepare for a meeting, but don't overprepare

Preparing for a meeting is important. It sets the stage for a productive discussion, gets everyone aligned on objectives and helps avoid that awkward moment where someone asks, "So, what are we here to talk about?" But while preparation is necessary, overprepping can be counterproductive. There's a fine line between being well-prepared and wasting time going over every possible scenario for hours:

- **Use an email to prepare for everyday meetings:** For informal catch-up meetings or routine check-ins, a well-written preparatory email suffices, so long as it covers the basics, such as who we are meeting, what we need to know about them, what we are hoping to achieve and any potential sensitivities we should bear in mind. This saves time and gives everyone a chance to review and prepare on their own schedule. Offer a quick call if someone has questions or concerns.

- **Hold a short preparatory call:** If your team is meeting with people from outside your organization, a preparatory call for team members can help. In the call, go over the basics, noted above, and outline team members' roles in the meetings. Often, a 15-minute call is sufficient for this. There's no need to turn it into a 60-minute deep-dive or hold multiple preparatory sessions, especially if the meeting isn't particularly high stakes or if the topic is familiar to you and your team. Spending hours going over every potential scenario can make you rigid and less adaptable to the natural flow of the conversation. It wastes time, too.

- **Prepare more for complex meetings:** For complex or high-stakes meetings—major client negotiations, strategic planning sessions or dealing with a client crisis—by all means, spend more time on the preparatory call or hold several calls, if needed to get every detail right. But still be ready to adapt in the actual meeting.

Ultimately, trust your team's expertise and experience. Prepare enough to feel confident and informed, but don't get bogged down iterating on minutiae.

Research who you are meeting

If you are meeting with someone or a group of people for the first time—for example, a potential new client—getting a quick sense of who they are is no longer optional, and it's easy to do in today's world of LinkedIn profiles and other social media. This prep work will reward you with valuable insights that can establish common ground and shape the conversation.

If you're meeting a team, it may be enough to do this background check simply on the leader, but the tips below include guidance on researching other members of the group:

- **Start with LinkedIn:** Nine times out of ten, the person you're meeting will have a LinkedIn profile. Use this as the first stop on your research journey. Confirm their current role and areas of focus by reviewing the "About" and "Experience" sections. These often provide useful details about their career trajectory, areas of expertise and any recent changes to their responsibilities. Pay attention to any new roles they've taken on, because this can offer timely insights into what they might be focused on currently. Skimming through their posts can reveal topics that interest them, allowing you to tailor your conversation accordingly. Don't forget to check for shared connections, particularly if they are strong connections of yours, because this can serve as an excellent conversation starter or a way to build rapport.

  But don't send a LinkedIn connection request before you've met the person. It's better to wait until after the meeting, then use the "Add note" feature in the connection request to make it personal. Reference your conversation and thank them for their time; this reinforces the relationship and makes your connection request feel genuine.

- **A simple Google search can yield additional information:** You might find recent presentations or events they've participated in, which often offer insights that aren't available on their LinkedIn profile. If they've written articles or been featured in interviews, these can provide deeper understanding of their perspectives, interests and background. These resources are especially useful when meeting senior leaders, because they often have shared their strategic viewpoints or professional values in public forums.

- **Research others who will be in the meeting:** It's most important to check out the leader, but researching other in the group can give you a sense of what perspective each one might bring to the meeting as well as their company's organizational structure and potential power dynamics. For example, if several people from different departments are involved, understanding their roles and how they interact within their organization can help you navigate the conversation more effectively. Knowing the reporting structure may give you insight into how decisions are likely made and where each person stands in the corporate hierarchy.

Note: Keep in mind when using LinkedIn that if the person you looked up is a frequent user of the platform, they may notice you've looked them up. This isn't a bad thing—it often signals professionalism and preparedness—but it's good to be aware of it.

Think carefully about what pre-read or meeting materials to require

Too frequently when people convene meetings, they seem to be operating on the assumption that more meeting materials equate to better outcomes, but in reality, they can often be a distraction, slowing the meeting down and wasting time. And as for pre-reading, it's important to weigh the benefits the materials provide against people's busy schedules and the likelihood they will, in fact, read the materials in advance.

Limit materials for smaller meetings or forgo them

For a smaller meeting with a purpose such as discussing a new report or product, materials may be warranted so that the details can be clearly understood and referenced during the conversation. For example, survey results can be shown through well-designed visualizations, and product features can be highlighted. The question is how much material is appropriate. For an hour-long meeting, a slide deck or report with 20–35 pages is overkill. Curate the materials down to the most essential pieces. Don't be tempted to overload an appendix; ironically, by design, you're signaling this material is nonessential and at best, only the first few pages will be skimmed.

A telltale sign your materials may be unnecessary or overly long is when a colleague—often someone senior who isn't creating the meetings—says, "It's okay if we don't get through all the materials; they'll be a good item to leave behind for them to read later." This is a red flag. If the materials are seen as less essential before the meeting, then they likely aren't needed at all—or at the very least, they are too long. Challenge yourself and your team to critically assess whether the materials are essential or could be significantly shortened.

A more informal or routine meeting, such as a catch-up session, often does not require any materials at all. In fact, materials in these settings can get in the way of meaningful dialogue. Instead of relying on slides or handouts, focus on a personal, organic conversation where the participants are free to engage fully without distractions. However, you still need to verbally lay out an agenda at the beginning of the meeting to anchor the discussion and keep it focused.

Only send pre-read materials when they will significantly improve a meeting

These materials typically fall into two categories: preprepared materials (such as a new report or product marketing content) and purpose-developed materials created specifically for the meeting. When it comes to preprepared materials, only send them ahead of time if you have a strong belief recipients will actually read them. If you suspect they won't get read, it's better to share them in the meeting or as a follow-up. This way, the conversation remains focused and the materials can be reviewed at participants' convenience.

Materials developed expressly for the meeting require a more thoughtful approach because they are a substantial effort. If you believe the participants will benefit from reviewing such materials in advance—particularly if the materials will help set the stage for a more informed discussion or energize the meeting—then they make sense. However, if they are more of a nice-to-have than a must-have, skip them. The time spent creating and reviewing such materials can be better used elsewhere if they aren't truly adding value.

When sending materials out in advance, timing is important. For shorter documents, send them two or three days before the meeting. This serves two purposes: it acts as a reminder that the meeting is approaching, and it provides participants enough time to review the content without feeling rushed. For longer, more complex materials, follow the "weekend-plus-two-day" rule: make sure recipients have at least a weekend plus two business days to review. For example, if the meeting is on a Monday, send the materials on the previous Wednesday. For a Thursday or Friday meeting, send them the prior Friday. This approach provides participants with flexibility to review either during the workdays or over the weekend, so they have sufficient time to prepare.

Help junior colleagues prep for success; don't just throw them in

When it comes to their responsibilities regarding junior team members and meetings, too many managers and senior colleagues believe their role is simply to offer opportunities for leadership or speaking roles. "It's a great chance for you," they say, and consider their job done. This approach, commonly referred to as "sink or swim," assumes people will learn by jumping into the deep end. As a nonswimmer myself, I've always rejected this mentality. Expecting someone to succeed without the right preparation isn't just risky—it's unfair.

Listen to your junior colleague practice and offer constructive feedback

Helping junior colleagues prepare thoroughly is a worthwhile investment. When you turn over the running of a meeting or presentation to them, take the time to guide them through the process—but avoid simply dictating how you would approach it. Instead, let them walk you through their plan for the meeting. Encourage them to explain how they will structure their message, handle questions and engage the audience. This builds their confidence and allows you to more effectively assess their readiness.

As they present their plan, take detailed notes. When you offer feedback, avoid prescribing your own method. Instead of saying, "Here's what I would do," ask guiding questions like "Have you considered addressing issue X?" or "How will you respond if Y happens?" Framing your feedback this way encourages them to think critically and refine their approach.

Make sure to emphasize that although they should consider your feedback, they must deliver the presentation or lead the meeting in their own voice and style. If they merely mimic you or adopt a script that doesn't feel authentic to them, it will be evident and the meeting may fall flat. Remind them that they're not there to be you—they're there to be the best version of themselves, using their own strengths and personality to lead effectively.

> "Take advantage of every opportunity to practice your communication skills so that when important occasions arise, you will have the gift, the style, the sharpness, the clarity, and the emotions to affect other people."
>
> — Jim Rohn, entrepreneur and author

Offer additional support, feedback and congratulations

Preparation support shouldn't be limited to meetings you attend. It's equally valuable to help someone prepare for a meeting you won't be attending. If you are attending the meeting, continue to support their growth by observing and taking notes. Pay attention to what they say and to how they engage the room, respond to challenges and manage the flow of the conversation. After the meeting, offer a balanced debrief. Highlight what went well and offer suggestions for improvement in a way that encourages development. For example, "You did a great job staying on track despite the disruptions. If something similar happens again, you might consider proposing a follow-up meeting to give more attention to topics that didn't get enough airtime."

If you didn't attend the meeting, check in with them afterwards. Ask how it went, what challenges arose and how they felt about their performance. This shows that you are invested in their growth, not just in the success of the specific meeting. Regardless of the outcome, always take the time to congratulate them for stepping up. Acknowledge the effort they put into preparing and leading and thank them for embracing the opportunity.

Know how to start and run a meeting

> "Meetings are at the heart of an effective organization, and each meeting is an opportunity to clarify issues, set new directions, sharpen focus, create alignment, and move objectives forward."
>
> — Paul Axtell, consultant and writer

Leading a meeting requires your active facilitation, focus and ability to guide discussions effectively. Your role is to keep the conversation on track, encourage balanced participation and drive toward clear decisions and actionable outcomes. This begins with starting on time, making meaningful introductions, managing the agenda and keeping the conversations at the right level.

Be on time

In a time where back-to-back Zoom or Teams calls are the norm, being punctual is more important than ever. Most of us have days when we're scheduled from morning to evening with barely a minute to breathe between meetings. But showing up late to meetings, whether they're virtual or in person, is disrespectful and disruptive. Don't tell yourself that it's okay to be four our five minutes late to a call or meeting you accepted. It isn't. Arriving five minutes late is even more disrespectful in our post-COVID world, where everything seems to run on 30-minute meetings. Five minutes are a significant percentage of a 30-minute meeting.

Instead, adopt these habits:

- **For virtual meetings, join early, if you can:** Join a minute or two early, if possible. This shows that you're prepared and ready to engage from the outset. It gives you a moment to settle in, check your audio and video settings and maybe even catch up with colleagues before diving into the agenda.

- **If you're late, apologize, but don't ask to be caught up:** It's frustrating for those who were on time to have to recap what's already been discussed just because you didn't make it on schedule. Join quietly, listen closely and piece together what you missed. Most of the time, you can catch up without needing a full recap. If there's something you truly don't understand, unless it's critical, make a note and ask about it after the meeting rather than interrupting the flow for everyone else.

- **If you struggle with punctuality, improve how you manage your schedule:** Factor in a few minutes between meetings for a mental reset or for transitioning from one call to the next. If you're running from one meeting to another with no buffer, it's no wonder you're late. Consider booking meetings for 25 or 50 minutes instead of the full half-hour or hour. This gives you and your colleagues a little breathing room and increases the likelihood that everyone shows up on time for the next call or meeting.

Invest time in introductions

In a world of back-to-back meetings, we often feel the urge to jump straight into the agenda and get down to business. However, if you're leading a meeting, whether virtual or in-person, invest time in proper introductions. Some may see this as a formality or a time waster, but a few minutes spent letting participants introduce themselves sets the stage for a more open and inclusive dialogue. It allows people to share a bit about themselves and fosters a sense of mutual respect. When people skip introductions, it can make a meeting feel cold, missing the human touch that helps build relationships:

- **Let individuals introduce themselves:** Too often, senior figures or meeting facilitators rush through introductions on behalf of others. While this may seem efficient, it robs people of the chance to establish themselves in the room. We all know ourselves best and can introduce ourselves better than anyone else can. Having someone else perform the introduction can make the person being introduced feel as if their own words aren't as valued, which can discourage participation before the discussion even starts.

  Consider a situation in which a colleague has taken the time to prepare for an important meeting—dressed the part, prepared their materials and arrived with the expectation of contributing meaningfully. Then, a senior leader quickly introduces them on their behalf, rattling off their title or role without giving them a chance to speak for themselves. Imagine

your colleague's feelings in that moment. Letting everyone speak for themselves, even briefly, sends a powerful message: "You matter, and your presence here is valued."
- **Opt for brief introductions versus none:** There may be situations where time is genuinely tight and introductions need to be kept very brief. In those cases, quick introductions in which participants share their name, role and one key expectation for the meeting still creates a sense of inclusion without derailing the agenda. (See "Know how to introduce yourself and what you do," in Part 3).

When the meeting merits it, use the Chatham House Rule to promote candor

In meetings involving participants from multiple different organizations, participants can hesitate to contribute fully due to concerns about confidentiality or linking their name or the name of their organization to a particular view. This reticence can significantly limit the quality and depth of the discussion. One simple way to alleviate participants' concern is by explicitly stating that the meeting will operate under the Chatham House Rule.

Contrary to common misconception, there is only one Chatham House Rule (i.e., it's the Chatham House Rule, not Rules), and it states "When a meeting, or part thereof, is held under the Chatham House Rule, participants are free to use the information received, but neither the identity nor the affiliation of the speaker(s), nor that of any other participant, may be revealed."[3] The purpose is to allow for a free exchange of ideas without the worry of attribution, encouraging participants to speak more openly and share their true thoughts.

Under this approach, participants are permitted to share what they've learned, but with some restrictions. For example, it's acceptable to say, "I attended a meeting of industry experts last week to discuss climate change and heard that companies are confused by new government policies." It is not acceptable, however, to reveal who made the comments or their affiliations. While it's not explicitly forbidden, it's also best to avoid mentioning who attended the meeting to prevent any potential inferences about attribution.

Some organizations adopt a modified version of the Chatham House Rule that permits participants' names and organizations to be listed in follow-up reports or discussions while keeping their specific remarks anonymous. This modification is typically used to lend credibility to a meeting's outcomes or final reports. However, if this is to be the adopted approach, participants should be informed of this adjustment ahead of time. Springing it on them at the start of the meeting can lead to discomfort, especially for those who expected the meeting to offer full anonymity.

If you took the time to prepare an agenda, lay it out first before diving in

> "Meetings without an agenda are like a restaurant without a menu."
> — Susan B. Wilson, business writer

An agenda serves as a road map that helps everyone understand the meeting's approach and objectives. It provides clarity on how the discussion will unfold, allows participants to mentally prepare for each item and opens the door to potential adaptations before the discussion begins:
- **Outline the agenda without getting lost in detail:** If you've taken the time to create an agenda (and you should), make sure to lay it out at the beginning of the meeting, before diving

---

[3] "The Chatham House Rule," Chatham House, Royal Institute of International Affairs, 2024.

into the content. This reduces the likelihood of someone interrupting later in the meeting to ask if a particular topic will be covered. When you give an overview of the agenda, stay at the summary level. Avoid the tendency to jump ahead and start front-running the entire discussion. Too often, people start presenting an agenda and immediately go deep into the second or third agenda item—often because it's the topic they feel most comfortable with or the one they are most passionate about. While understandable, this can derail the meeting before it even gets started and overwhelm participants with too much information up front.

- **Once the agenda has been presented, be open to adjustments:** There are times when someone—especially a senior person or an important stakeholder—may suggest reordering the agenda items or adding a new point that wasn't originally included. If that happens, be flexible. This accommodating approach fosters a sense of collaboration and shared goals and helps focus the meeting on what's most important to the group as a whole, not just the person who created the agenda. Agendas are not rigid scripts; they are tools for guiding discussion. If it makes sense to shift the order of items based on the needs of the group, don't hesitate to adapt. Just make sure any changes are agreed upon by the group and everyone understands the revised flow of the meeting.

  Be careful not to abandon the agenda entirely, however. There's a balance between being flexible and letting the meeting get completely sidetracked. If a change is requested, quickly evaluate whether it serves the overall purpose of the meeting and whether it will still allow you to hit the key objectives. If it does, go ahead and make the adjustment. If not, explain the reasoning for sticking to the original plan and offer to cover the additional point either later in the meeting or in a follow-up conversation.

- **Consider weaving the news into the meeting introduction:** For example, if you're leading a discussion on supply chain issues, finding a recent article on supply chain disruptions or shifts in the global market will show that what you're discussing is part of a larger, real-world conversation. It gives the meeting a sense of urgency and highlights to participants that the topics being covered are not just theoretical but are affecting the industry or world in around them.

- **Take a moment, if appropriate, to say a word about the meeting space:** If you're meeting at a historic building, a well-known hotel or an exclusive club, you can add depth and meaning to the occasion by tapping into the history or significance of the location. Do a bit of research on the venue beforehand. This could be as simple as checking the hotel's website or reading about the building's history in a local guidebook. You may find an interesting anecdote, a famous event or a notable person associated with the location.

  A former senior colleague of mine had a real talent for this. No matter where we met, he would always find a way to tie the venue's story into his opening remarks. For example, he might start a client meeting by saying, "We're meeting today in a building that once hosted some of the most pivotal negotiations in the city's history—what better place for us to come together to tackle these challenges?" Words like these seize participants' attention and remind them that they are part of something special.

"The stronger person is not the one making the most noise but the one who can quietly direct the conversation toward defining and solving problems."

— Aaron T. Beck, psychiatrist and developer of cognitive behavioral therapy

Needless to say, if you're leading the meeting, you have an even greater responsibility to maintain the meeting's schedule. For timekeeping, rely on a clock or a wristwatch rather than your phone, because looking at your phone can give the impression that you're checking emails or otherwise disengaging from the conversation. You may even suggest that all meeting attendees turn off their phone and keep them out of sight as a way of reducing distraction and promoting engagement. One of my former colleagues used to bring a small, foldable clock to larger meetings. This clock looked official, reinforcing his role in keeping the meeting on time and served as a visual cue to the group that he was monitoring the schedule.

Maintain the right altitude in the discussion

Finding and maintaining the right altitude in a meeting—that is, a balance between strategic and detailed discussions—is one of the most challenging aspects of meeting management, and part of your responsibility if you are leading the meeting. When experts and specialists are in the room, there's always a risk of diving too deep into the weeds because their specialist knowledge means they excel in the details, but if a meeting becomes bogged down in minutiae, the broader objectives can get lost:

- **Determine the desired level of discussion:** The first step to managing the right altitude is determining what level of discussion is needed based on the meeting's objectives. Are you there to focus on broad, strategic trends and implications, or are you tackling specific, detailed issues? Is the meeting for informing participants or to make decisions? The purpose of the meeting will dictate the altitude at which the discussion operates. If it's a high-level strategic meeting, it should stay focused on trends and decision making. If it's more detail oriented, you'll want to zero in on specific issues, but not lose sight of the overall goals.

- **Actively manage the meeting to maintain altitude:** Constant calibration is necessary to keep the meeting at the right level, but has to be done in a natural, energizing way. You don't want to come across as overly rigid or corrective. Avoid phrases that sound dismissive or critical, like "We've gotten off track," which can stifle productive dialogue and frustrate participants. Rather, you might say, "That's a valuable point; let's schedule a follow-up to dive into that. For now, let's return to the main topic." This acknowledges the importance of detailed discussion but reinforces the need to stay focused on the meeting's core purpose. One useful technique is the "parking lot" method, where you note detailed or ancillary issues for later follow-up without allowing them to derail the main discussion.

By actively guiding the discussion and maintaining a clear sense of the desired level of focus, you can help participants stay engaged and contribute meaningfully without getting lost in unnecessary detail.

Know how to manage question-and-answer segments

Question-and-answer (Q&A) segments are a specialized type of questioning that happens in formal group meetings and presentations. (For more on asking questions and questioning generally, see "Use questioning and active listening for deeper engagement" in Part 3.) Q&A segments can become rushed and unproductive, but the following guidance can help you avoid the pitfalls:

- **Set expectations for the timing of the Q&A segment:** If the agenda allows for 15 minutes of questions, the chair should explicitly state this to participants: "We have 15 minutes for questions." This simple statement signals to everyone the time is limited and helps participants understand not every question will get asked.

- **Outline how questions will be handled:** Will the chair take one question at a time, or will they group several questions together? Handling questions serially—one at a time—allows for deeper answers but often results in fewer questions being asked. Taking multiple questions at once gets through more questions but can lead to overly brief answers and requires respondents to remember several unrelated questions, which can be difficult. It's also possible to use both approaches: the chair can start by taking one question at a time and, if time runs short, can group related remaining questions for more streamlined responses.

- **Determine how questions will be directed:** Will the chair ask every respondent to answer each question or will they direct specific questions to particular individuals? It will likely be a mix. Some questions will naturally lend themselves to a spectrum of responses from multiple participants, while others will be best answered by one specific person. By clarifying this approach early on, the chair can prevent a situation where every respondent feels obligated to weigh in on every question, a practice that is overly time consuming and limits the number of questions that can be addressed.

- **Make sure the audience knows what questions are asked:** For larger meetings or events, it can be hard for everyone to hear the questions being asked. If the room has microphones, the chair should encourage participants to use them. If not, the chair should repeat each question after it's asked, so everyone knows what it is (this also gives respondents a little extra time to formulate their answer, which can lead to more thoughtful and articulate responses).

The chair may want to have prepared questions or planted questions ready to go (see "Have some prepared or planted questions," below). These questions can jump-start the session and encourage others to ask follow-up or related questions.

Know how to manage interpersonal dynamics in meetings

In addition to whatever urgency or tension surrounds the issues under discussion at a meeting, there are the tensions and emotions that arise because you've collected a group of people, all with their own perspectives, goals and motivations, in one place. If you're leading a meeting, there are several things you can do to keep sparks from flying and to channel energy and emotions toward productive outcomes.

Stay focused on being the chair, not a participant

Large meetings need a designated chair to keep them on track and prevent them from losing focus or becoming unproductive. If you find yourself in the role of chair, it's important to understand that this position comes with both responsibilities and limitations:

- **Actively steer the meeting:** As the chair, your primary obligations are to set the context for the meeting, guide the discussion through the agenda, facilitate participation from all attendees and conclude the meeting with clear next steps. While this may sound straightforward, it's often more difficult than expected. For example, even with careful planning, sometimes getting through the first half of an agenda takes longer than anticipated. This is due to natural human dynamics—some topics spark longer discussions than planned. As the chair, it's your responsibility to keep the meeting on track, managing time while respecting the flow of conversation.

- **Adapt the agenda, when required:** As discussed earlier, you should be ready to adapt the agenda should it be necessary—as in the case described in the previous point, when the first half has taken longer than expected. With experience, you will learn the types of topics that can be deferred if needed to keep the meeting on schedule.

- **Be circumspect in offering your own views:** The most challenging part of being a chair is managing the constraints of the role. A former colleague once said that the best chairs are the ones who know more about the topic than anyone else in the room, but use that knowledge to guide the discussion, not dominate it. As chair, you have to be careful not to state your own views too often. While you don't have to be completely silent, you must remain impartial. Your goal is to encourage others to contribute, especially if they have conflicting perspectives or fresh insights.

Your contributions as a chair should be limited and purposeful, helping move the discussion forward rather than curtailing or controlling it. Striking the right balance between facilitating and participating can be difficult, but it's a necessary skill, and with practice you will become accomplished at it.

Don't let someone commandeer the meeting

When your team has organized a meeting—spent the time preparing and agreeing on approach, flow and everyone's roles—there's nothing more frustrating than having a colleague completely disregard it all within the first five minutes of the actual meeting. You know the situation—you've set up the agenda, discussed who's leading which parts, agreed on key messages and even laid out protocols like "don't jump in immediately" or "let's avoid offering opinions too early." Then the meeting starts, and suddenly, one or two people decide to run the show their own way, completely ignoring what was decided in the preparatory session. When this happens, it creates confusion and can make your team look disorganized or uncoordinated. This is especially damaging in high-stakes meetings—for example, with a potential client or investor, where impressions matter and mixed signals can lead to missed opportunities or lost credibility.

If you've agreed to a meeting approach, stick to it. It's okay to be flexible and adjust as the meeting evolves, but make those adjustments thoughtfully and as a team. If the situation calls for a change in approach—for example, if the client wants to focus on a different matter or new information comes up that changes the context—pause and in the moment quickly realign with your team. A simple, "Hey, do we need to adjust our approach based on this?" can do wonders. It shows you're adaptable but still respectful of the groundwork that was laid.

If you find that a colleague regularly deviates from the plan, it's time for a candid conversation. Approach it as a learning opportunity, not an accusation. "Hey, I noticed we went off-script in the last meeting. Can we talk about what happened?" Maybe they felt the situation called for it or weren't as bought into the plan as you thought. Understanding why they strayed can help improve future preparations. It's also an opportunity to reinforce with them the fact that such behavior is damaging to team morale and shouldn't happen routinely.

"Because meetings involve people, things can and will go wrong. Provide first aid when necessary."

— Emily M. Axelrod, writer and cofounder of the Axelrod Group consultancy

---

Know how to balance speaking time so meetings are inclusive

In any meeting, whether it's 10 or 20 people, there's a risk that three to five participants will dominate the conversation. This reflects a combination of personality types, knowledge and seniority. While this dynamic is common, there are ways to work against it to make meetings more inclusive. The following purposeful and proactive strategies can amplify other voices:

- **Manage the seating arrangement:** Where possible, position the more vocal members on the periphery of the room or to the side of the chair. While this latter tactic may seem counterintuitive, it allows the chair to use subtle verbal and visual cues—like eye contact or a light touch on the arm—to gently signal when it's time for these participants to hold back and allow others to contribute. But it can also work to put quieter members near the chair (or directly across from the chair), because this can make it easier for the chair to draw them into the discussion. Placing quieter members closer to the chair also gives those members higher visibility, which may make it easier for them to engage.

- **Bring up participants' known views on a topic:** If the chair has insight into people's perspectives or expertise on a subject, they can invite those individuals into the conversation to share their views. For instance, the chair might say, "Soren, we've discussed renewables previously, and I know you have some valuable perspectives. Would you mind sharing them with the group?" This approach validates the participant's expertise and opens space for them to speak.

- **Invite junior members of the team to participate:** This can be done in a way that doesn't feel abrupt or forced. As in the previous strategy, the chair can ask a more junior participant to contribute based on their specific knowledge or work; for example, "Caden, since you pulled together the latest survey, could you summarize the key findings for us?" This provides them an opportunity to speak on familiar content and helps them build confidence in their public speaking and presentation skills.

But be careful not to force inclusion for its own sake. The goal of an inclusive meeting isn't to have everyone speak or have equal airtime. That would quickly become awkward and lead to artificial, heavy-handed interventions by the chair. Instead, the objective should be to create an environment where everyone feels comfortable participating and knows that inclusion is valued.

Get comfortable with interrupting

In everyday life, interrupting people or constantly cutting them off is considered rude. But in the context of a well-run meeting, interrupting sometimes is both acceptable and necessary. Meetings are meant to be collaborative and inclusive, but as noted above, there are sometimes moments when someone grabs the proverbial microphone and dominates the conversation. In these moments, the meeting chair or other senior participant should interrupt so the conversation remains balanced and productive:

- **Interrupt firmly with apologies:** Interrupting in these moments should be direct without being rude. A simple, "Marc, apologies for interrupting, but I think Debra has something to add here" shifts the conversation and opens the floor to others. The person you interrupt may initially bristle at being cut off, but often they're simply caught up in the flow of their own thoughts and don't realize how much time they've taken. In most cases, they'll understand that the interruption wasn't personal but was made to keep the meeting balanced and on track.

By tactfully stepping in, you're demonstrating that everyone's input is valued and that no one person should dominate. When meeting participates realize that the chair will intervene to maintain a varied conversation, they are more likely to remain attentive and engaged.

The art of interrupting is partially about timing. If you wait too long, the rest of the attendees may become disengaged, and it may be difficult to pull the meeting back on track. On the other hand, if you interrupt too soon, you risk creating tension or coming off as heavy-handed or controlling. Ideally, you can step in when the speaker has reached a natural pause or when it's clear that the speaker's point has been made and it's time to move on.

- **Bring the interrupted person back into the discussion:** This is a good way to mollify them and keep them from feeling sidelined or unappreciated. You circle back and say something like, "Marc, earlier you mentioned X. I'd love to hear more about that now." This gesture shows that their input is still valued and helps smooth over any potential frustration they might have felt at being cut off. It reengages them in the conversation and provides them with another opportunity to contribute.

Handle interruptions gracefully

The other side of interrupting is when you are the person who is interrupted, or when one meeting participant interrupts another. Interruptions are an inevitable part of conversations and meetings, but how you handle them can significantly affect the flow of discussion and how others perceive you. Handling the situation well shows professionalism and maturity.

If you are the chair and one meeting participant interrupts another, take a moment to assess the situation. People may interrupt out of enthusiasm or because they feel they have an important point to add. If the interruption seems well-intentioned, let the person finish their thought, but then invite the original speaker to continue. If someone is constantly cutting others off, step in with tact: "Lisa, let's allow Yesel to finish and then we'll hear from others." This addresses the issue and signals to others that their voices matter.

If you're the one who's interrupted, stay composed. Avoid visibly reacting with frustration or anger, which can derail the discussion or create an awkward atmosphere. Instead, maintain eye contact, remain calm, let the person finish their main point and then use your words to regain control of the conversation. For example, you might say, "I'd like to finish my thought before we move on" or "I hear you, but let me complete this point first."

Use silence to elicit engagement; it really is golden

In professional settings, especially during meetings or discussions, many people find silence deeply uncomfortable. You've likely experienced it: someone has spoken, they seek a response and then… nothing. Just silence. The quiet that follows can feel endless, particularly in large groups where you might expect more people to jump in. But here's the truth: the hours of silence you experience in your head are mere seconds in real time. Get comfortable with it.

Silence is a powerful tool for fostering thoughtful discussion and engagement. It allows time for reflection, for participants to gather their thoughts and for those who might be more reserved to consider their responses. Not everyone processes information at the same speed, and some people prefer to think longer before they speak.

The discomfort silence provokes is also a subtle motivator, because it can spur someone to step forward with a thoughtful comment or question. It's especially valuable in larger groups, where people may hesitate to jump in because they don't want to interrupt or dominate the conversation.

If you are chairing a meeting and you know you get uncomfortable when meetings are silent, before intervening when a silence takes hold, try counting in your head. Most of us feel the urge to fill a silence after just 10 or 15 seconds. Instead, count to 45 or even 60 seconds before stepping in to speak. You'll likely find that by then, a meeting participant will have taken the initiative to contribute. They just needed the space and time to do so. By holding off, you will have given the room time to breathe, leading to richer, more meaningful dialogue.

"Well-timed silence hath more eloquence than speech."

— Martin Farquhar Tupper, poet and novelist

Have some prepared or planted questions

Although silence can often be enough to provoke people to speak, another effective technique for facilitating discussions, redirecting conversations or encouraging participation in meetings is to use prepared or planted questions. Such questions help maintain the flow of dialogue, make sure key points are covered and help engage quieter participants:

- **Be ready with questions to transition to the next topic:** As chair, when you see that a topic has been exhausted, use a question to lead into the next topic. For example, if the discussion about risks presented by a project has gone on for too long, say something like, "We've covered the risks in depth. What opportunities does this project present?" This shifts the focus smoothly while acknowledging the prior conversation. It's better than simply saying, "Let's move onto the next topic," which can feel abrupt and suggest a lack of continuity from one topic to the next.

- **Make judicious use of planted questions:** Planted questions involve prearranged participation from others in the meeting. As chair, you discreetly ask a participant before the meeting to raise a certain question at an appropriate time. Your prompt is something subtle, such as "Does anyone have any questions?" rather than an overt cue like "Carol, you had something you wanted to ask, right?"

To be most effective, it's good for the questioner to provide some context or offer an initial perspective along with the question. This enriches the discussion.

Know how to conclude a meeting

The endings of meetings are as important as the beginnings. If the meeting chair is to carry through on the responsibility to guide the meeting to a satisfactory conclusion, that goal must be kept in mind from the very start. Recapping can help attendees recognize all that's been accomplished, and reviewing next steps carries the momentum forward. And, just as starting on time is important, so is finishing on time.

Drive towards the decisions and outcomes you desire

> "You have a meeting to make a decision, not to decide on the question."
>
> — Bill Gates, cofounder of Microsoft and the Gates Foundation

Every meeting should have a clear purpose and desired outcome or set of outcomes, which should guide the agenda and management of the meeting. The following tips can help a meeting stay on track:

- **State the objective up front:** The chair should state the meeting objectives in their opening remarks to remind everyone of the reason for the meeting and what it is hoped will be accomplished.

- **Make focusing on meeting objectives a shared responsibility:** A good chair reminds attendees that keeping the meeting on track is a responsibility shared by all participants. Every attendee should exercise self-restraint and keep their contributions on topic. True, if participants drift off course or dive too deep into unnecessary details, the chair may step in and redirect the conversation. However, participants can help keep the meeting focused by proactively suggesting adjustments to the agenda if they notice time is slipping

away or fear that key matters may not get the attention they deserve. Passively waiting for the chair to fix the agenda undermines shared accountability.
- **Call attention to achievements:** After discussion on an agenda item concludes, the chair should recap what has been achieved in the context of the intended outcomes before moving on to the next topic. This makes the conclusion of discussion on the topic explicit and provides participants with an opportunity to clarify or correct any misunderstandings. At the end of the meeting, the chair should perform a final, overall recap, reiterating what was achieved.

If you put "next steps" on the agenda, get to next steps

In almost every meeting I've attended over the past two decades, when there's an agenda, "Next Steps" is listed as the final item, typically with five to 10 minutes allocated for it. This segment is to summarize what's been agreed upon during the meeting and to outline the concrete actions that need to be taken afterward. However, a significant number of these meetings never actually get to the next-steps portion. Instead, they're hurriedly mentioned in the final 15 seconds with a remark like "We'll send around a list of next steps." This translates to "Oops, we didn't have time for this." Not surprisingly, often the next steps are forgotten or overlooked.

That is regrettable, because next steps are critical. It's at the next-steps stage that the discussions and decisions made during the meeting become tangible actions that can move the issue or project forward. Without next steps, the meeting is just another conversation, and participants leave without knowing exactly what is expected of them. It jeopardizes execution of agreed-upon tasks.

If you are the meeting chair, be intentional about managing the time spent on earlier parts of the agenda. Keep an eye on the clock so you leave enough time to discuss and agree on next steps. If you find yourself consistently running out of time for next steps, consider agreeing on and documenting them at various points in the agenda.

Assign someone to take notes during the meeting, specifically focusing on action items and next steps. This can be a dedicated notetaker or a role rotated among the team. The important thing is that someone is documenting agreed-upon actions as they're being discussed. This helps make sure nothing is missed when, as chair, you state what you recall regarding next steps. The notes also become a record of shared accountability when they are shared after the meeting. Each recorded next step should include key decisions made, deadlines, who is accountable for each action to be taken, follow-up checkpoints and, when appropriate, resources required, dependencies on other actions to complete the next steps or potential obstacles. You can use an action-tracker document to track completion of next steps over time and to inform agendas for subsequent meetings.

Use mind maps to recap a meeting

Mind mapping is a powerful tool for summarizing discussions, especially when the meeting covers multiple topics or subtopics. If you are the chair, you can use it to structure a concise and accurate recap when the meeting draws to a close:
- **During the meeting, jot down topics and subtopics:** The key to using mind maps is staying high level. Keep a blank page in front of you specifically for the mind map. As the dialogue starts, begin by writing down the first topic that comes up. Maybe it's artificial intelligence, so you write down "artificial intelligence." This is your first cluster. As subtopics are discussed, start adding short bullet points around that central label—for example, "impact on workforce" and "needs responsible guardrails." The idea is to capture the essence of each part of the conversation without getting bogged down in the specifics. You're creating a visual reminder that can guide you later when you do a recap.

When a new topic comes up in the discussion—risk management, for example—create a second cluster called "risk management" on the mind map and repeat the process, jotting down bullet points for the subtopics, such as "data bias" and "regulatory requirements." As the conversation flows and revisits earlier topics, simply add new bullets to the appropriate cluster—for example, you may return to the first cluster and add "need for reskilling." The mind map will grow organically as the meeting progresses.

- **Avoid detailed notetaking:** Avoid the temptation to write full sentences. Writing whole sentences will slow you down and shift your focus from actively listening to documenting the conversation. Stick to bullet points and keep them brief—just enough to jog your memory when you need to explain the main points later.

- **Disengage from the meeting to map out your summary:** Five minutes before you're due to give a recap, disengage slightly from the ongoing conversation to review your mind map. Quickly number the clusters, either based on the order in which the topics came up or from most to least important. The number of bullets around each cluster or the amount of time spent on each topic should give you a good sense of what was emphasized during the meeting.

By numbering the clusters, you create a road map for your recap. When it's time to summarize the meeting, you can quickly move through the topics in an organized, logical way. A good mind map allows you to provide a coherent overview, hitting the main points without having to sift through pages of traditional notes.

End a meeting on time

When the allotted time for a meeting or call is up, recognize that fact and end the discussion as planned. Too often, people say, "I want to be respectful of your time," only to continue the conversation for another five or more minutes. That's the opposite of being respectful—it disregards the time limit that was set and is inconsiderate the fact that participants have other commitments to attend to.

If you reach the end of a meeting's allotted time and there's still more to discuss, resist the temptation to continue. Instead, acknowledge the time and clearly state that the meeting will conclude. For example, you could say, "We're at the top of the hour, so let's wrap up. We'll schedule a follow-up to cover the topics we didn't discuss." This demonstrates you value everyone's time and shows you'll be proactive in arranging another meeting to address remaining matters.

If you find yourself consistently running over, it might be time to reassess your meeting-management skills. Perhaps you are putting too much on the agenda, not doing enough prior to meetings to get participants aligned or not actively managing the meetings to get through the agenda efficiently. If you're running the meeting effectively and all the issues on the agenda need to be covered, then you may need to schedule longer meetings.

If a meeting ends early, don't feel pressured to fill the remaining time just because it was scheduled. If all the key points have been covered and the objectives met, go ahead and wrap up early. Your colleagues will appreciate the extra time back in their day, and it reinforces the idea that your meetings are focused and efficient.

Be prepared for the unique challenges of virtual meetings

Virtual meetings and conversations have become commonplace since the pandemic. Yet, without the benefit of physical presence and body language, managing these conversations effectively can be challenging. With the right techniques, however, virtual conversations can be as engaging and productive as face-to-face meetings:

- **Set a clear agenda:** It's true for in-person meetings, and it's especially true for virtual meetings. Agendas keep the conversations focused and efficient.
- **Facilitate active participation:** In virtual meetings, it's easy for some participants to fade into the background. As the host or key participant, encourage active participation from everyone by asking open-ended questions and calling on quieter participants by name. For example, "Toni, what are your thoughts on this?"
- **Keep conversations concise and focused:** Without the in-person energy and body language cues, virtual conversations can easily drift or lose focus. Try not to let that happen. Be clear when moving from one topic to the next and summarize key points as you go. For example, after discussing a particular issue, you could say, "To recap, the key takeaways are A, B and C. Does anyone have anything else to add before we move on?" This keeps the conversation moving and everyone aligned.
- **To the degree possible, be mindful of body language and nonverbal cues:** Even though in virtual meetings the most we can generally see is our fellow participants' heads and chests, that still offers us certain nonverbal cues, like facial expression and posture. Direct eye contact can be tricky—people tend to look at their screen rather than the camera—but when you're speaking, try to look into the camera to simulate eye contact. This small effort can help others feel more engaged, and they may follow your lead. Encourage participants to turn on their cameras to foster stronger connections and reduce distractions. Pay attention to those who keep their cameras off, but be understanding—there can be circumstances that require it (e.g., if they're working from home and have a toddler who needs to be attended to).
- **Use technology to your advantage:** Take advantage of the tools virtual platforms offer to increase interactivity and productivity. For instance, use screen sharing to visually guide participants through key points or documents. Use breakout rooms if the conversation needs to be split into smaller, more focused discussions. Polls and reaction features can help gauge the room's sentiment and keep engagement levels high.
- **Manage audio and avoid interruptions:** Audio quality is crucial in virtual conversations. Encourage all participants to mute themselves when they're not speaking to minimize background noise. If someone does get cut off or experiences technical difficulties, acknowledge it and give them a chance to finish their thought. Interruptions can feel more jarring in a virtual setting, so be patient and avoid talking over others. It can help to encourage everyone to use visual cues, such as raising a virtual hand or using the chat function, when they have something to contribute.

As noted below with in-person meetings, it's important after the conversation to follow up with a concise summary of the key points discussed and the actions assigned. This provides clarity and creates accountability.

Know how to follow up on meetings

Professional follow-up helps round off meeting and calls attention to key points and actions, especially for meetings with stakeholders from outside your organization. Follow-up can take many forms, but it should be clear, actionable and timely:

- **At a minimum, follow up with a brief message of thanks:** This type of follow-up is mainly for informal meetings where no substantial decisions or discussions took place, for example, a professional networking event. For example, you might send out an email saying, "Thank you for attending the meeting. We trust you found it valuable. [We/I] look forward to seeing you next time." While brief, such a note acknowledges the participants' time and contribution and closes the interaction on a polite note.

- **Highlight specific contributions:** A more personal follow-up notes some contributions made during the meeting, highlighting why they stood out. For instance, "I thought [your/another person's] point on industry consolidation was particularly insightful. Until then, it felt like everyone was dancing around the issue." This type of message shows you listened to and valued the recipient or others' views, and it builds a foundation for future discussions.

- **Document substantive points to inform future meetings and enable wider dissemination:** For more formal meetings or those with substantive discussion points, a more detailed recap can be beneficial. This could be a list of three to five bullet points summarizing key topics, conclusions or decisions made during the meeting. If next steps were agreed upon, these should be included. A well-crafted follow-up helps participants recall what was discussed and, if appropriate, enables them to share the takeaways with colleagues without having to write their own notes. This type of follow-up is especially useful after meetings that are part of a series because it provides continuity and means important points are carried forward into future discussions. (Note: these summary emails do not replace the need for formal minutes in official meetings.)

Timeliness in follow-up demonstrates professionalism and organization. Ideally, follow-up emails should be sent within 24–48 hours of the meeting, when the meeting is still fresh in participants' minds. Sending a follow-up a week after the meeting can give the impression that the meeting wasn't particularly important or that follow-up was an afterthought, which can diminish people's commitment to future meetings.

*****

Mastering the art of meeting management means your discussions are productive, inclusive and respectful of everyone's time. By focusing on preparation, timekeeping and maintaining the right tone, you guide meetings toward meaningful outcomes. Now, let's dive deeper into advanced conversational techniques, where we'll explore how nonverbal cues, storytelling and active listening can elevate your conversations and help you build stronger connections in any business setting.

PART 3

Advanced Conversational Techniques

Part 3 delves into advanced conversational techniques, focusing on mastering nonverbal cues, effective questioning, accessible language, storytelling, creation of trust and conflict management. It emphasizes reading the room and knowing when to step up or step back in discussions.

In Part 3

- Master nonverbal dynamics.
- Use questioning and active listening for deeper engagement.
- Choose language that is easy to understand.
- Make your conversation memorable through stories and comparisons.
- Build trust through self-awareness and balanced dialogue.
- Handle conflict with confidence and clarity.

Master nonverbal dynamics

Mastering nonverbal cues in personal interactions can significantly elevate your presence and effectiveness in professional settings. How you present yourself—your dress and posture, the way you engage with others—often speaks louder than words. Learning to read body language, use eye contact and maintain a receptive, engaged posture will help you build rapport and strengthen others' impression of you.

Dress appropriately

Dress code can be a sensitive topic, especially in multicultural environments where there are different expectations for what is appropriate. Yet, how you dress significantly affects how you are perceived. To present yourself well and make a positive impression, be mindful of dress expectations and balance personal style with professionalism.

The first step is determining whether your organization or client has an official dress code. Typically, such policies outline what's explicitly not allowed (for example, shorts, sandals or overly casual attire) and provide guidelines for appropriate attire, such as business formal for client meetings or business casual for everyday office wear.

Unfortunately, while prohibitions are easy to follow (you're told what not to wear), vague guidelines, such as "business casual," are often open to interpretation and leave room for confusion. What exactly is business casual? For men, it usually means no tie is required, but what about jackets? In more formal business settings, jackets are often still expected, while in more casual settings, a vest or well-tailored sweater may suffice. For women, the ambiguity is often even greater—what's equivalent to a man's jacket without a tie? The line between casual and business casual can blur, adding further complexity. Casual attire might allow for jeans, but what kind? Are polo shirts or sneakers appropriate? The answer varies by organization.

In practice, there's often an unwritten dress code—a norm that goes beyond the official guidelines. Some clients or organizations may allow business casual but prefer a more formal appearance, especially in certain settings or industries. Observing or asking about the typical dress norms can help you dress appropriately. For instance, while a technology company might allow sneakers, an old-school financial institution might still expect formal shoes.

Ultimately, you have to decide how you want to be perceived. Matching your work attire to the norm isn't conformity for conformity's sake; it's about demonstrating professionalism and commitment to the organization's culture. In most cases, investing in quality, well-fitting business attire is never a bad decision. Clean, tailored clothes project confidence and professionalism, and being well-dressed generally leaves a positive impression.

But be mindful not to overdo it. Showing up in all designer or custom-made attire without considering the environment may send unintended signals of privilege or wealth that could create discomfort. Strike the right balance between dressing to impress and being inadvertently boastful or overwhelming.

Know how to introduce yourself and what you do

In Part 1, we discussed the importance of knowing how to tell your backstory. You should know how to use that narrative to craft a relevant and concise introduction that leaves a strong impression. The particulars of that self-introduction will depend on your tenure, seniority and role:

- **Junior colleagues or new hires should focus on their role:** If you're new to the workforce or only a few years out of college, you may have little experience, so it's tempting to note your education or recent graduation. Instead, focus on your role within the team. For instance, say, "I'm part of the project team focused on risk reporting," and, if appropriate, mention the person you support, such as, "I'm supporting Kathryn and her team." Avoid using titles that don't translate well outside the organization or that emphasize your junior status. Saying, "I'm a consultant" is much better than "I'm a junior consultant" or "Staff One." The goal is to highlight your value and to avoid underselling yourself.

- **Senior colleagues should balance pedigree and expectations:** If you're more senior, you will naturally have more to say, but brevity and clarity are still important. Depending on your title, you may need to clarify your role. The title of CFO may be self-explanatory, but in other cases, providing context is helpful. For example, instead of saying, "I'm the head of data analytics," try "I lead the team that uses customer data to improve our products." This approach makes your role more relatable and highlights what you do.

When introducing yourself, be mindful of how you present your background. For example, while you may be proud of your long tenure at an organization, overemphasizing it might signal resistance to change or innovation. Conversely, listing too many past roles or employers can come across as trying to prove you know everything, which can be off-putting. Instead, focus on introducing yourself in a way that explains your current role, what you hope to contribute to the meeting and what you're hoping to learn from the discussion (the latter element signals your willingness to listen and respect for others' views).

Regardless of your age and tenure, when introducing yourself, keep it brief. Avoid diving into long explanations or detailed insights that are better suited to the meeting itself.

Be confident, even when you aren't

> "Your success will be determined by your own confidence and fortitude."
> — Michelle Obama, attorney and wife of former president Barack Obama

A small minority of people you meet have genuine self-confidence. They are visibly comfortable in their own skin, walk tall and exude an ease that draws others to them. A lucky few individuals possess true charisma, which can be incredibly potent when experienced firsthand. The rest of us, however, don't have such deep stores of confidence to draw on. We are mere mortals, often dealing with self-doubt or even bouts of anxiety, especially in high-pressure settings—if we're leading a critical meeting, for example, or standing in front of 250 people at a conference. It's normal. If you sometimes feel unsure or inadequate, remember you're not alone.

Fortunately, you're not stuck with a fixed allocation of confidence—you can develop and cultivate it over time, using certain tools and techniques. For example, one technique is to prepare carefully before every important meeting. Review the agenda and read and digest the meeting materials. If you have speaking role, don't overwhelm yourself with pages of notes. Instead, condense your thoughts into five or six key bullet points, each no more than three or four words long, focusing on the core elements you want to convey. Rehearse these key points until they are second nature. Don't overload your mind with every possible detail—just the essentials you can easily remember. In the meeting, breathe deeply and deliberately slow your speaking. Keep focused on the most important points.

These tactics build confidence over time. A few years ago, a young colleague—on her third working day after college—stepped up to a whiteboard to summarize a complex discussion. She nailed it. She stood upright, spoke slowly and made a point to look around the room, engaging with everyone rather than just focusing on the whiteboard. While practiced, her behaviors didn't feel rehearsed or artificial.

That's the beauty of projecting confidence when it's done right: it feels natural, even though it may take deliberate effort and practice behind the scenes. It doesn't take years, but it does take some time.

Straighten your posture

Posture is important. Good posture offers physical benefits: standing or sitting up straight with your shoulders back and head held high improves breathing, reduces strain on your muscles and alleviates tension in your neck and back. This alignment boosts energy levels, helping you stay more alert and focused during the day.

Posture also plays a key role in nonverbal communication. When you stand tall, you project confidence and competence, making others more likely to trust and engage with you. Good posture supports strong eye contact and active listening, enhancing the quality of your interactions. Slouching, by contrast, can unintentionally signal lack of interest, fatigue or a lack of confidence, even if that's not how you feel.

> "A good stance and posture reflect a proper state of mind."
> — Morihei Ueshiba, founder of Aikido, a martial art

When thinking about posture, remember the following:

- **Small practices can make a big difference:** Standing up straight when walking or sitting with both feet flat on the ground can have a big impact. The advice of my father, a sergeant major, has always stuck with me: breathe in deeply, pull your shoulders back and look people directly in the eyes. These small adjustments project confidence and will help you feel stronger, even if you're not feeling it inside.
- **Exercises that strengthen your core muscles will also help:** Core exercises naturally improve your posture over time. A simple exercise for strengthening your upper back and improving your posture is the seated shoulder blade squeeze: sit up straight, squeeze your shoulder blades together as if holding a pencil between them, hold for 5-10 seconds

and repeat 10–15 times. To further enhance your posture, consider taking up yoga, which is excellent for building core strength and improving overall alignment.

Spell and say people's names correctly

One of the simplest yet most powerful ways to show respect and consideration for others is by spelling and pronouncing their names correctly.

It's easy to assume that minor errors—like writing Marc instead of Mark or Ann instead of Anne—don't matter, but for the person whose name is being misspelled, it can grate. The same principle applies to pronunciation. Names often carry cultural or familial significance. When you make the effort to spell or pronounce someone's name correctly, you're not just getting a detail right, you're acknowledging their identity and showing that you value them. On the flip side, consistently misspelling or mispronouncing someone's name can come across as insulting, even if it's unintentional:

- **Double check spellings in business communications:** Whether in emails, meeting agendas or presentations, check that you're spelling your colleagues' names correctly. Making an extra effort with accents or diacritical marks on letters (e.g., é, ñ or ç) will be especially appreciated and demonstrates even greater respect for the name.

- **If possible, discover how to pronounce a name before you need to say it:** If you will be introducing a speaker or reading out the names of award recipients, confirm that you know how to say the names. If there are any you feel unsure about, reach out to someone who can help you. The person in question is always the best source, if that's an option. Saying, "Could you help me with the pronunciation of your name?" or "How do you prefer your name to be said?" shows humility, respect and a genuine interest in addressing them properly. A helpful strategy is to write down the name phonetically, so you have a clear reference for the correct pronunciation. Repeat the person's name back to them, allowing them to correct you if necessary. Practice helps, especially for names you aren't accustomed to.

- **Avoid self-excusing advance apologies:** Avoid the common habit of saying, "I'm sorry, I may butcher your name," and then blundering ahead with a mispronunciation. While the intention of the remark might be to soften the error, it often only intensifies it.

Even with the best intentions, mistakes can happen. If you misspell or mispronounce someone's name, apologize and make a note so you don't repeat the mistake. Don't make it a big deal, but do make it clear that you're committed to getting it right.

Address people by name when you're talking to them

A subtle but effective communication technique is to use the name of the person you're speaking to a few times during your conversation with them. While it might feel unusual at first, addressing the person you're speaking to by name can increase their engagement in the discussion.

We're wired to respond to our names, and when someone uses it during a conversation, we feel seen, heard and acknowledged. When someone addresses us by name, the exchange feels more personal, even if the setting and subject are business related. The use of our name makes us feel more central to the conversation. Putting this technique into practice during a one-on-one meeting might sound something like this: "Aurora, I think we're aligned on the main objectives here," or "That's a great point, Aurora, and it ties into what we discussed earlier."

This technique personalizes interactions such as performance reviews, project updates or problem-solving meetings, fostering stronger connection among participants. It works especially well in virtual settings, where nonverbal forms of engagement or reassurance aren't available (or are much less available). On video or phone calls, it's easy to feel disconnected. Simply using someone's name can help reestablish and strengthen a connection.

Use this approach with care, however. Overusing someone's name can come across as insincere or, in some situations, aggressive. The key is to use their name naturally, with a light touch. In most one-on-one discussions, saying someone's name two or three times should be enough to create the desired effect without coming across as false.

Show interest in people and remember personal details that matter to them

One of the most important factors in building strong professional relationships is getting to know people on a personal level and remembering details about their lives. It demonstrates interest in them as people who have a life outside the workplace. Remembering personal details like where someone lives, their family situation or their hobbies can create a connection that goes beyond work interactions.

When you bring up personal details, it demonstrates care and thoughtfulness. Asking about a colleague's recent vacation or their child's graduation, for example, gives them a chance to share a positive memory. It brightens that moment and possibly their whole day. Don't overlook more challenging aspects of their lives, such as a family member's health or a recent bereavement. The goal isn't to dwell on difficult topics, but to show empathy and compassion.

Don't rush these personal conversations. If someone opens up about a tough time, take the time to listen, even if it cuts into the time you set aside for work-related discussions. These moments are crucial for building trust and rapport, and more fundamentally, are part of necessary human connection. Put yourself in their shoes: if you shared something personal and the person you were talking to immediately changed topic, how would you feel? Most likely, worse than ever. You'd be unlikely to trust the person with personal matters in the future.

When someone entrusts you with personal details, remembering them demonstrates the sincerity of your interest in them. However, if you work with many people, it can be hard to keep everything straight. Jotting down notes in a notebook or on the back of a business card can help. Just be mindful of where you store sensitive information. While it's fine to enter professional details like job changes in your organization's customer relationship management tool, do not log personal details about a client's family, health or other such matters. Keeping this information out of the organizational sphere prevents private information from being misused and helps maintain the trust you've worked hard to build.

Maintain eye contact

Eye contact is a crucial element of effective communication, yet for many, it can be challenging, especially in smaller group settings. You might notice that some people struggle with this—they fidget, look down at the table or focus on their notes, even while speaking. Though these actions might seem minor, they can unintentionally convey unpreparedness or a lack of confidence, which in turn erodes others' confidence in them.

- **Maintain eye contact when you're speaking:** This signals you're engaged and confident and builds connection with the people in front of you, making them feel like active participants in the conversation. Consciously meeting people's eyes projects confidence even if you're nervous. The person or people you're speaking to are more likely to trust you and your message.

- **Maintain eye contact when listening:** Eye contact reassures the speaker you're paying attention and validates their contribution. It demonstrates you're fully present and actively absorbing what the speaker is saying. Frequently breaking eye contact, by contrast, can signal distraction or lack of interest, even if that's not your intention.

   In smaller groups, maintaining eye contact can be more challenging because it involves engaging with multiple people. However, it is all the more important in these intimate settings—it builds trust and fosters open dialogue.

- **Use eye contact when delivering presentations to larger audiences:** If you're speaking to a large group, eye contact is still effective. As you scan the room, make direct, brief, eye contact with individual audience members. This makes everyone feel included, strengthening connections between you and the group. I once attended an event with more than 100 attendees at which former British Prime Minister John Major gave a speech. He used eye contact masterfully: even though he caught my eye for no more than a few seconds, it felt as though he was speaking directly to me for several minutes.

Making eye contact may take practice if it doesn't come naturally. Start by consciously practicing in low-pressure settings, like casual conversations with colleagues or friends, and gradually work up to more formal or larger group settings. The goal is to make your eye contact feel natural and engaging, not forced or uncomfortable.

Read body language and mood in the room

Knowing how to read body language and the mood in the room are essential skills. The nonverbal cues you can glean from people's body language offer valuable insights into how they are feeling, how engaged they are and whether the conversation is headed in the right direction:

- **Observe posture and positioning:** Start by observing how people are seated or standing in the room. Are they leaning forward with interest or are they slouched back in their chairs—which might signal that they are disengaged or bored? Open body language, like uncrossed arms and legs, generally indicates a positive, open mindset, while crossed arms or turned-away bodies suggest defensiveness or discomfort. Take note of these signs early in the meeting or conversation to get a baseline of how engaged people are, then monitor for changes as the discussion progresses.

- **Watch for eye contact:** This is one of the most telling indicators of engagement. If someone maintains steady eye contact, they're likely engaged and focused on the conversation. However, if you notice people are avoiding eye contact, frequently looking at their phones or gazing around the room, it may indicate boredom or discomfort. In group settings, watch who makes eye contact with whom—this can reveal power dynamics or alliances within the group. For instance, if a junior colleague frequently glances at a more senior colleague before speaking, it might indicate they're seeking approval or reassurance, highlighting a sense of hierarchy in the group or a sense of wariness about the topic under discussion.

- **Assess facial expressions:** Facial expressions are key to reading emotions and reactions in the moment. A furrowed brow, pursed lips or tight jaw can indicate confusion, frustration or disagreement. A smile or relaxed facial expression, on the other hand, signals comfort, agreement or openness. When presenting an idea or asking for input, check for subtle changes in facial expressions to gauge how well your message is being received. If you see confusion or discomfort, it may be a good time to ask, "Does anyone have any questions or concerns about what we've discussed?"

- **Monitor group dynamics:** Pay attention to how people interact with each other. Are there side conversations happening, or is everyone focused on the speaker? Side conversations can indicate disengagement or that there's an issue that needs addressing. If people are nodding in agreement or leaning toward one another, it suggests alignment. If you notice people avoiding each other's gaze or looking tense, it may signal disagreement or tension. Understanding these group dynamics can help you manage the flow of the meeting, allowing you to bring issues to light or steer the conversation toward resolution.

- **Be aware of energy shifts:** The overall energy of the room can shift during a meeting or conversation, so be attuned to those changes. If the energy is high—people are sitting up straight, nodding and contributing actively—it usually means the discussion is engaging and on track. However, if the energy starts to dip—people begin shifting in their seats, looking at the clock or becoming quiet—it's time to change tack. You might need to ask a thought-provoking question, introduce a new topic or take a quick break to reenergize the group.

- **Validate observations with verbal check-ins:** While body language and mood can provide important clues, it's important to validate what you observe by asking direct questions. For instance, if someone's arms are crossed and they haven't spoken much, you might say, "I'd like to hear your thoughts on this." Or if the room feels tense, ask, "It seems like there might be some concerns—what are we missing?" This allows you to address underlying issues and gives everyone an opportunity to be heard.

"A conversation is so much more than words, a conversation is eyes, smiles, the silences between the words."

— Annika Thor, novelist and screenwriter

Guidance on reading body language

Type	What it reveals	Positive sign	Negative signs
Facial expressions	Reveal emotions, attitudes and reactions.	Smiling, relaxed facial muscles, eye contact.	Frowning, clenched jaw, avoiding eye contact.
Smile dynamics	Indicate sincerity and warmth, or nervousness or masking depending on the type of smile.	Genuine smile that reaches the eyes.	Forced or half-hearted smile, smirking or a tight-lipped grin.
Gestures	Reinforce, supplement and sometimes replace spoken communication, expressing opinions and emotions.	Nodding, signaling approval (e.g., giving a thumbs up, pointing and nodding), signaling with hands for the speaker to continue.	Shaking the head, crossing arms, clenching a fist on the table, pointing aggressively.
Posture	Indicates state of mind.	Upright and relaxed posture, leaning slightly forward.	Slouching, leaning away, crossing arms or legs tightly.

Type	What it reveals	Positive sign	Negative signs
Eye contact	Demonstrates attention, interest, confidence and sometimes challenge. Note: How much eye contact is considered appropriate varies by culture.	Consistent yet natural eye contact (not fixed stares), relaxed gaze.	Avoiding eye contact, staring intensely, blinking rapidly.
Proxemics (personal space; i.e., how close to others a person stands)	Reveals level of comfort. Note: How much space people should give to others varies greatly between cultures.	Maintaining situationally and culturally appropriate personal space.	Standing too close or too far (but see note: sometimes this can simply be a matter of unfamiliarity with the culture).
Mirroring (i.e., copying another person's behavior)	When done unconsciously: alignment, rapport; when done consciously or exaggeratedly: possible mockery, hostility.	Natural and subtle mirroring.	Conscious, obvious or exaggerated mirroring.
Unconscious hand movement	Nervousness, tension; may also indicate neuroatypicality.[4]	Although potentially distracting for others, not all hand movements indicate something negative; sometimes they merely indicate a greater inability to keep still.	
Feet position, unconscious foot movement	Signals comfort or discomfort; unconscious foot movement may indicate neuroatypicality.	Feet flat on the ground, pointing towards the conversation partner.	Tapping feet, shifting weight, pointing feet away from the speaker (but see note regarding neuroatypicality).

Offer, don't seek, credit

All people appreciate recognition for their work. Being the person who's generous in offering that recognition rather than seeking credit for yourself will build up a store of gratitude and admiration and can improve the workplace climate. Desiring recognition for one's own hard work is understandable, but attempting to gain recognition through self-promotion—by highlighting one's own contributions—often backfires, creating friction and undermining relationships. True leadership and influence come from a mindset of lifting others up and celebrating their successes:

- **Avoid credit-seeking behavior:** Constantly highlighting your own role can alienate your peers and tarnish your reputation. When colleagues sense that you're more focused on claiming the spotlight than promoting team success, they'll be less inclined to collaborate or engage with you, which will ultimately diminish your effectiveness and could lead to missed opportunities for genuine recognition.

- **Offer credit proactively and strategically:** Make it a habit to recognize the contributions of your colleagues whenever they have a meaningful impact. Whether they led a project, provided valuable insights or supported the team in important moments,

---

[4] The term "neuroatypicality" refers to variations in neurological functioning, such as autism, attention deficit hyperactivity disorder (ADHD) and related conditions. These variations may result in behaviors like unconscious hand or foot movement, which are not necessarily indicative of nervousness or discomfort but may reflect unique cognitive or sensory processing. Understanding these nuances encourages inclusivity and reduces misinterpretations in communication.

acknowledging their efforts fosters goodwill and builds a culture of appreciation. Instead of offering vague compliments like "Great job," be specific: "Soren's analysis refined our strategy and helped us make data-driven decisions." This level of detail lends credibility to your praise and highlights your colleagues' particular contributions. Seize opportunities to commend colleagues' achievements during meetings, particularly when senior leaders are present. Again, be specific in your praise: "Caden did an excellent job distilling our meeting materials down to what really matters," calling attention to their work's tangible value. But in a team situation, remember that too much praise for one person can lead to resentment on the part of other team members. A light touch is best. Recognizing various team members over time maintains positive dynamics and keeps anyone from feeling overlooked.

- **Acknowledge clients in front of their team:** When working with clients who have made significant contributions to a project's success, take the opportunity to praise their efforts in front of their senior leaders or team members. Publicly linking your success to their actions reinforces your partnership and shows that you genuinely appreciate their work. As with any compliment, make sure your praise is sincere and well-timed—exaggerated or insincere remarks can be quickly spotted by perceptive executives, undermining your credibility.

Lighten the mood with humor

There are a growing number of articles and TED Talks touting the benefits of laughter in the workplace, linking it to higher performance, better mental health and a host of other positive outcomes. Laughing triggers the release of dopamine and endorphins—our body's natural feel-good chemicals—that reduce stress and increase motivation.

The simple truth is that laughter makes work and life better. Who doesn't enjoy walking away from a meeting or call where everyone shared a smile or a good laugh? Moments of humor break up the monotony of the workday and create a sense of camaraderie. You're more likely to look forward to calls or meetings that you know will have some lightheartedness.

When we laugh together, barriers come down. People feel more comfortable speaking up and more able to share ideas and even admit mistakes. An atmosphere in which laughter is possible is one in which people can be their authentic selves. No surprise, teams that laugh together often perform better.

So, how do you bring laughter into your work setting without it feeling forced or fake? The good news is, you don't have to be a comedian or the office clown. Just appreciate the lighter side of life and be willing to share it. It starts with being able to laugh at yourself—acknowledging the occasional awkwardness or irony that comes with any job. Maybe you make a self-deprecating joke when you realize you've been on mute for the first 30 seconds of your presentation, or you share a funny anecdote about a mishap that ended well.

Be open to humor from others and encourage light-hearted moments, even in serious settings. If someone cracks a joke, don't be the person who reminds everyone of the need to stay on track. Let those moments breathe. Work is a big part of life, and life is better when you can smile.

But recognize the limits to where and when humor can be deployed. Some meetings aren't meant for jokes, and some cultures may view humor as inappropriate. Gauge the mood of the meeting and use your judgment to decide when and how to bring levity into the room.

"Wit is the salt of conversation, not the food."

— William Hazlitt, essayist and philosopher

Use questioning and active listening for deeper engagement

Effective questioning and active listening are fundamental to productive conversations. Knowing how to ask the right questions and listen actively helps you draw out valuable insights, sustain engagement and guide conversations toward meaningful outcomes.

Just ask the question—don't preface it with "I have a question"

A pet peeve of mine is when people preface their inquiries with "I have a question." It's unnecessary. Unless you're in a setting where airtime is hard to come by, there's no need to announce that you have a question—just ask it.

Questions are essential in any professional environment. They elicit clarifications and further information; they challenge assumptions and deepen the discussion. However, starting with "I have a question" halts the natural flow of discussion and calls unnecessary attention to the act of questioning. By simply asking your question outright, you convey confidence and show that you're actively engaged and ready to contribute. The conversation flows more naturally.

There's an important caveat, however. If you notice team members frequently preface their questions with "I have a question," it might be worth exploring why, because it may signal that they're struggling to be heard. When people feel overlooked or find it difficult to gain the group's attention, they may announce their questions more formally, in effect saying, "Please give me space to speak!"

If you are the meeting leader, work hard to create an environment where everyone feels comfortable contributing. If you notice people often using "I have a question" as a prelude, reevaluate how inclusive your conversations are and take steps so everyone has space to speak and preludes become unnecessary.

> "There are no foolish questions and no man becomes a fool until he has stopped asking questions."
>
> — Charles Proteus Steinmetz, mathematician and engineer

Ask questions that open up the conversation

The questions we ask play an important role in the conversation. Good questions open up discussions, encourage collaboration and invite different perspectives. On the other hand, poorly framed questions stifle conversation and shut down meaningful engagement. Although open-ended questions are generally more desirable, there can be a place for closed-ended (yes-or-no) ones too. A good mix, with the right type employed at the right time, leads to better dialogue:

- **Use open-ended questions:** To encourage conversation and deeper thinking, ask open-ended questions rather than questions that elicit a simple yes-or-no response. Start your questions with "how" or "why." For example, instead of asking, "Do you agree with our current approach?" ask, "How do you see this approach fitting into our current strategy?" Instead of "Does this app make sense for us?" ask "Why do you think this app hasn't been adopted in our context yet?" These types of questions invite the other person to share their thoughts, insights and perspectives.

Yes-or-no questions are especially unhelpful when they seem intended merely to elicit approval. After presenting your ideas for several minutes, asking, "Does that resonate?" forces the listener either to agree with you or risk being a contrarian. If, instead, you ask, "How do you think we could build on that idea?" or "What would you add to what I've said?" your questions signal you're not seeking validation, but meaningful input.

- **Use closed-ended questions when appropriate:** Yes-or-no questions are desirable when you need to confirm or rule something out, such as "Did we hit our planned deadline?" or "Is the system back online?" In those situations, you don't want discussion; you merely need a piece of information.

"The best scientists and explorers have the attributes of kids! They ask questions and have a sense of wonder. They have curiosity. 'Who, what, where, why, when and how!'."

— Sylvia Earle, marine biologist and explorer

Guidance on types of closed-ended questions

Type	Description	Best use	Examples: artificial intelligence (AI)
General yes/no	Requires a straightforward yes or no response to confirm or deny a statement.	To quickly obtain confirmation or negate a simple fact or assumption.	Is AI currently being used in our email marketing campaigns?
Leading yes/no	Subtly encourages the respondent to agree with the interviewer's perspective.	To build consensus or subtly direct the conversation in a desired direction.	Wouldn't you agree that AI could significantly enhance our client communication strategy?
Dichotomous	Presents two mutually exclusive options, asking the respondent to choose one.	To guide the respondent towards a specific choice or direction.	Would you describe our AI communication tools as effective or ineffective?
Multiple-choice	Offers multiple predefined options, asking the respondent to select the best fit.	To categorize responses or streamline decision making by limiting options.	Which AI application do you believe has the most potential: chatbots, natural language processing or automated content?
Fact-based	Seeks factual information that can be quantified or verified.	To extract precise data or quantitative details relevant to the conversation.	How many AI-driven customer interactions do we manage each day?
Scale	Asks the respondent to rate or rank their level of satisfaction or agreement on a scale.	To measure satisfaction, preference, or opinion in a quantifiable manner.	On a scale of 1 to 10, how satisfied are you with the performance of AI in our communications?

Guidance on types of open-ended questions

Type	Description	Best use	Examples: artificial intelligence (AI)
Exploratory	Encourages broad thinking about a topic, focusing on possibilities and future trends.	When exploring new ideas, identifying opportunities or considering future possibilities.	How might AI transform the way we approach client communications in the future?
Clarification	Seeks to gain a better or deeper understanding of something under discussion.	When complex material is being discussed, or when the conversation is overly vague.	What do you mean when you say AI could personalize our customer interactions?
Probing	Aims to uncover specific details or additional information related to a topic.	To dig deeper into issues, uncover challenges or gather detailed insights.	What challenges have you encountered when integrating AI into communication channels?
Reflective	Invites the respondent to reflect on the reasons behind their thoughts or actions.	When seeking insight into motivations, thoughts or decisions made by others.	You prefaced you remarks about the proposed AI interface with 'If it actually works as advertised.' Can you expand on your doubts or worries?
Comparative	Encourages comparison of two or more ideas, approaches or methods.	When comparing alternatives or evaluating different options and approaches.	What are the benefits of AI-driven communications as compared to traditional methods?
Opinion solicitation	Asks the respondent's opinion or viewpoint on a specific topic.	To understand the personal perspective or beliefs of the respondent.	In your view, what role should AI play in shaping customer experiences?

Engage others in the discussion early on

We've all been on calls in which three or four senior people dominate the conversation, while other participants remain largely silent. Then, at the last minute, someone realizes there's a whole group of others on the call who haven't said a word. These people—who often lack senior titles—have been sidelined. The most frustrating part? This could have been easily avoided by opening the call to these others early on with a simple question: "What do you think?"

Long monologues are difficult to interrupt, even if people have valuable insights—something to bear in mind if you're one of the senior people on the call. If you talk for 10 minutes straight without pausing, others may feel their opportunity to engage has passed. A better approach is to break your presentation into smaller segments, interspersing open-ended questions throughout.

One of the most infuriating calls I've ever been on involved a senior client—a call we'd spent ages coordinating. My colleague, who was leading the call, monopolized the entire hour without once inviting the client or anyone else to contribute. At the 59th minute, he realized how staggeringly rude and counterproductive it was to dominate the conversation, leaving no room for others to speak. That was the last call I ever did with him. The lesson is simple: don't be that person.

If you are one of the senior people, before the meeting even begins, make a conscious effort to think about when and how to invite participating colleagues—especially more junior or quieter team members—to contribute. Don't wait until the end, after another senior person or group of them have already taken all the airtime. Build space into the discussion early on for different voices to be heard, especially those who might not naturally jump in. Asking "What do you think?" is fine, but more specific questions can be even better. For example, you can ask, "How do you see this affecting your team?" or "What questions does this approach raise for you?" These questions encourage participation that will enhance the meeting overall.

This approach is especially important when dealing with clients or external stakeholders. A client who spends an hour listening to you or your team talking nonstop will likely leave the meeting feeling unenthusiastic and unheard, even if the content was relevant. Inviting their input throughout the conversation, not just at the end, signals you value their perspective and are invested in a two-way dialogue. It also gives you the opportunity to correct course mid-conversation if the client's needs or expectations differ from what you anticipated.

Practice active listening

Active listening can transform the way you engage with colleagues, clients and other stakeholders. It goes beyond simply hearing what someone says—active listening involves fully concentrating, understanding, responding and remembering. In addition to maintaining eye contact and using open-ended questions, discussed earlier, active listening includes several other elements:

- **Eliminating distractions:** To listen actively, you need to give the speaker your full attention. Silence your phone and put it out of sight, close your laptop and, if possible, avoid taking extensive notes while someone is speaking. This will keep your focus entirely on the conversation at hand.

- **Focusing on the speaker's words, not just your response:** A common mistake in conversations is thinking too much about how you'll respond to what someone is saying rather than truly listening to the speaker. If you're busy formulating a response, you're probably not contemplating fully all the implications and facets of what the speaker is saying. Listen with the intent to understand, not to reply. This can be especially challenging in fast-paced meetings, but try to take a moment to process what's being said before jumping in. If something is unclear, ask for clarification. You might say, "Can you elaborate on that point?" or "Did I understand correctly that you meant...?"

> "Don't just be usin' the time that I'm talkin' to be thinkin' 'bout what you're gonna say next."
>
> — Lornette "Mace" Mason in *Strange Days* (1995)

- **Avoiding interrupting:** It can be tempting to jump in with your thoughts or solutions, but interrupting disrupts the flow and devalues the speaker. Let the speaker finish before responding. If the conversation veers off course, gently guide it back without cutting them off. You might say, "That's interesting, but could we return to the point we were just discussing?"

- **Using nonverbal cues:** With active listening, your body language helps convey your focus on the speaker. Nodding occasionally, keeping eye contact and repositioning your body in the direction of the speaker show that you're engaged and processing what's being said. Be mindful of your posture, as noted earlier, to convey attentiveness.

- **Paraphrasing and summarizing:** Demonstrate active listening by paraphrasing or summarizing the speaker's points at appropriate moments. This shows that you're listening and confirms mutual understanding—or gives a chance for the speaker to clarify. Speakers do not always express themselves as clearly as they think, and hearing their ideas restated can help them notice any gaps or confusion. For example, after someone explains an idea, you might say, "So what you're suggesting is…" or "If I'm hearing you correctly, your main concern is…" This paraphrasing also prompts others to reflect on what has been said.

- **Reflecting back:** Reflective listening takes paraphrasing a step further by addressing the emotions or underlying concerns that the speaker may not have explicitly stated. If someone seems frustrated, you could say, "It sounds like this situation has been stressful for you." This demonstrates empathy and helps the speaker feel heard, fostering a more open and constructive conversation.

Create space for real-time and reflective thinkers

To foster a culture of inclusive and thoughtful discussions, it's helpful to recognize and accommodate the different ways people process information. Some people are real-time thinkers, who gain energy and clarity by engaging with ideas immediately, while others are reflective thinkers, who need time to process information before forming their thoughts. You should make room for both styles:

- **Understand the strengths of each thinking style:** Real-time thinkers excel in fast-paced discussions, contributing immediate opinions and actively shaping the conversation as it unfolds. Their quick-thinking style is valuable during brainstorming sessions or when decisions need to be made rapidly. Reflective thinkers, on the other hand, often deliver more considered and strategic insights because they take the time to thoroughly analyze and process information. Their thoughtful approach helps refine ideas and contributes to making sound, well-grounded decisions.

- **Create an inclusive dialogue environment:** If you lead a team or facilitate a meeting, structure the conversation to welcome both styles. Start by encouraging real-time thinkers to share their thoughts openly, allowing their energy to set the stage for lively discussion. But then intentionally create space later in the discussion to incorporate the insights of reflective thinkers, after they've had time to digest the information. Taking this approach signals that both types of thinker are valued and that contributions at any point in the discussion are important to the team.

- **Facilitate balanced contributions:** If you notice quick thinkers dominating the conversation, actively draw out reflective colleagues by asking the sorts of open-ended questions discussed earlier. Also, be mindful of your own thinking style: if you are a quick thinker, model making room for reflective thinkers, and if you are reflective, model speaking up. By modeling balanced participation, you will help guide the group toward a more inclusive discussion.

- **Make balanced decisions:** Avoid letting either thinking style dominate the discussion or decision-making process. Encourage real-time thinkers to view their initial ideas as starting points that can evolve with further input. Remind them that while rapid opinions are valuable, they need to remain flexible as new perspectives are added. Similarly, for reflective thinkers, make it clear that while their input is welcome at any stage, follow-up discussions may be necessary to incorporate their ideas, especially if they are shared after the meeting. Let them know that taking time to think doesn't mean they have the last word, but rather that their insights are part of a continuous dialogue.

Let people tell their go-to story, even if you've heard it before

As people gain experience, they often develop a set of well-practiced stories that they enjoy telling (in "Become an effective storyteller," you're encouraged to do the same). These stories, often witty or poignant, have been refined over time and storytellers rarely tire of sharing them. Even if you've heard one of these stories multiple times, it's important to let the person tell it again. This social grace and kindness contributes to goodwill and mutual appreciation.

When someone starts telling their go-to story, listen intently and avoid interrupting, even if you know it will be long. Acknowledge the humor or significance in the narrative and reflect on the main point they're making. If the story provides a new insight or perspective, say so, especially if it's a portion of the story you hadn't heard before. You don't need to offer excessive praise, but showing genuine appreciation for the story can strengthen your connection with the storyteller.

A critical rule: never interrupt with "You've told me this story before." Doing so signals impatience and implies that the storyteller is forgetful, which can quickly sour the conversation. Allow them to enjoy the moment of sharing their well-rehearsed tale because it's likely something they take pride in. Listening respectfully maintains a positive atmosphere and demonstrate your respect for the storyteller's experiences.

Know how to revive a dying conversation

Conversations have a natural life span, but sometimes they wither prematurely. In professional and social settings alike, knowing how to revive an ailing conversation is a valuable skill:

- **Ask open-ended questions:** A flagging conversation is another situation in which open-ended questions come in handy. If the conversation is dying prematurely, you might try asking a question that gets your conversation partner or partners to look at the topic from a different perspective. For example, if you're talking about planning an office party, you might ask what things make a party especially memorable. A question like this, which sparks reminiscences, may also open up new topics.

- **Listen for clues and follow up:** Sometimes the key to reviving a conversation lies in something one of the other participants has already said. Listening closely to their words can give you clues for follow-up questions. For instance, if the conversation has been about vacations, but has flagged after someone made a remark about being on a limited budget, you can tactfully shift the conversation by asking about locations of interest nearby.

- **Shift the topic naturally:** If a topic has been exhausted but it's desirable to keep the conversation going, gently shift to a new topic by making a connection between what's been said and something else likely to be of interest. For example, if you've been discussing work projects and the conversation slows, you might say, "Speaking of teamwork, I read an interesting article recently about the challenges in driving collaboration in remote environments—have you developed any practices that work?"

- **Share a personal story:** Sharing a relevant, personal anecdote can reinvigorate a conversation. It doesn't have to be overly detailed—just something light that relates to the current topic. For example, if the discussion is about work travel, you could mention an experience from one of your recent trips. Especially if your story brings up an issue or difficulty, it may inspire others to share something similar.

- **Use humor or light remarks:** Sometimes a little humor can turn a fading conversation around. A light-hearted joke that you make can inspire your conversation partner(s) to recall one of their own, and that buoyant atmosphere can help float the conversation for longer.

- **Know when to end gracefully:** While sustaining a conversation is important, it's equally important to know when to wrap it up. If your best attempts to keep the conversation going are being met with monosyllables or only brief answers, it's likely time to bring the interaction to a close with a polite exit. Depending on the situation, you can say something like "I've really enjoyed our chat; let's talk again soon," or "I don't want to monopolize your time; I know you [or you all] have other people you need to talk to, but this has been a pleasure." Whatever the circumstance, include an expression of gratitude.

Learn how to take notes effectively and unobtrusively

Active listening can be enhanced by note taking, but taking notes can be challenging when you're leading the discussion, especially in smaller, more intimate meetings with two or a handful of people. In those situations, it's important to maintain eye contact to reassure the participants that you're fully engaged in the conversation. As noted earlier, eye contact signals that you're actively listening, positions you as a peer and conveys respect to the person you're conversing with. Constantly looking down to take notes can give the impression that you're not committed to being fully there in the moment, so keep your notes concise. Focus on capturing only the most essential points. Limit yourself to writing two or three words for each agenda item, subtopic or key decision. These short prompts will serve as reminders when you draft more detailed notes later—but not too much later. Try to write them up within 24 to 48 hours, while the conversation is fresh in your mind.

"The more content you try to capture during a lecture or a meeting, the less you're thinking about what's being said."

— Ryder Carroll, designer and inventor of the bullet journal

Choose language that's easy to understand

Too often, people overengineer the way they speak, especially in professional settings. The result is dialogue that is torturous to follow, sometimes impossible to understand and almost always too long-winded. The problem is compounded when people try to sound overly academic or use corporate jargon—it's not natural; it's not how people talk to each other in daily interactions.

Your goal in any conversation should be to get your point across clearly, not to impress others with complicated words or phrases. A good rule of thumb is to pause before you say something and ask yourself: is this word or phrase going to sound awkward? Would I ever say this in a conversation with friends or family? If it feels forced or overly formal, it probably is. If it sounds pompous or silly in your head, it's going to sound that way out loud, too.

"The most valuable of all talents is that of never using two words when one will do."

— Thomas Jefferson, third US president and author of the Declaration of Independence

---

Use simple words and limit or eliminate overused or specialized language

In professional settings, people often use longer or more complicated words in an attempt to sound knowledgeable or sophisticated, but this can backfire: your message becomes harder to understand, and you can end up being less engaging. I once heard someone tell a colleague to "de-densify" a presentation slide. While their intention was clear—they wanted their colleague to make the slide less cluttered—using "simplify" would have conveyed the message more directly and with less confusion. Sometimes, using complicated words, jargon or clichés or foreign-origin terms can have the even worse effect of making you appear less trustworthy, as if you're hiding behind language.

When in doubt, opt for words that are straightforward and universally understood. Your audience will appreciate it, and simple language will keep the focus on the message itself:

- **Avoid turning nouns into verbs:** A common habit in business discussions is turning nouns into awkward-sounding verbs when we already have perfectly good verbs for the purpose. For example, in place of "We need to action this project," a simpler and clearer alternative would be "We need to implement this project." Using straightforward verbs instead of awkward noun-verb hybrids maintains clarity and keeps your language natural sounding.

- **Avoid overusing "-ize" words:** Business language is full of words ending in -ize that can often be replaced with simpler alternatives. Overusing words like "prioritize," "monetize" or "finalize" can complicate what you're saying. Instead of saying "We need to prioritize customer satisfaction," you can say "We need to focus on customer satisfaction." Or instead of "We plan to monetize this service," you could say "We plan to earn revenue from this service." Putting things in simpler language helps you yourself stay clear on what you're saying, which is important.

> "Eliminate the unnecessary so that the necessary may speak."
> — Hans Hofmann, abstract expressionist painter

- **Avoid clichés:** Overused phrases like "low-hanging fruit" and "reinvent the wheel" don't add clarity or value to your message; they merely make it feel stale and generic. Instead of saying "let's circle back," you could say "let's revisit this later." Similarly, rather than saying "peel the onion," say "analyze in depth." Replacing clichés with more direct and thoughtful language will make your message feel more fresh.

- **Avoid sporting metaphors:** Sporting metaphors, such as "knock it out of the park" or "call an audible" may be common in business settings, but they can alienate those unfamiliar with the sports in question. Instead of saying "keep your eye on the ball," try "stay focused on the goal." Similarly, rather than saying "step up to the plate," you could say "take responsibility." Avoiding sports-related phrases will help make your communication accessible to everyone, regardless of their familiarity with sports.

- **Use plain English instead of foreign-origin terms:** Foreign-origin terms, even common ones like "bona fide" or "quid pro quo," can alienate those who happen not to know the term in question. The less common the term, the greater the likelihood of alienating your listeners. Opt for plain English instead. For example, instead of "bona fide," say "genuine" and replace "quid pro quo" with "mutual exchange."

- **Avoid corporate jargon:** Corporate buzzwords can make a simple message impenetrable. While you may toss around the terms "actionable" or "synergy" all the time among your work peers, replacing them with alternatives such as "practical" or "cooperation" will make what you're saying more intelligible when you're speaking with someone from outside the organization. This is especially true if you're speaking to someone who's not in business. Even common corporate jargon like "leverage" can be hard for someone to understand if they're not in business and don't know the term.

> "The shorter and the plainer the better."
> — Beatrix Potter, author-illustrator and naturalist

Avoid overstating or overqualifying your remarks

Both overstating and overqualifying can reduce listeners' trust in what you're saying. By contrast, direct, well-grounded assertions will make you come across as both confident and credible:

- **Avoid hyperbole when emphasis is required:** It's tempting to grab attention with far-reaching promises or powerful adjectives, but when you overstate something, your claims may be hard to believe, or you may create unrealistic expectations, leading eventually to disappointment. Instead, use precise and appropriate language to convey your point. For example, rather than saying, "Our new feature is revolutionary," you could say, "Our new feature significantly enhances user experience." Similarly, instead of "This product is failproof," opt for "This product is highly reliable."

- **Avoid weakening superlatives:** Superlatives like "best," "perfect" or "unanimous" have set meanings. Weakening them with qualifiers like "almost" or "nearly" reduces their effect and clarity. If you're not confident enough to use a superlative without a qualifier, it's better to choose a different word altogether. For example, instead of saying, "The project is nearly complete," say, "The project is 95% finished." Similarly, rather than saying, "We had virtually unanimous support," state, "Eleven of the twelve board members supported management's proposal."

- **Eliminate superfluous modifiers:** Words like "really," "actually," "basically" and "literally" clutter your commentary and weaken your message. Removing these unnecessary modifiers makes your language more direct and powerful. For instance, instead of saying, "We are really behind schedule," simply say, "We are behind schedule." Instead of "We are basically over budget," say, "We are over budget." These small changes will sharpen your statements and make them more effective.

- **Avoid preambles and uninformative qualifying statements:** Preambles like "It goes without saying" or "For all intents and purposes" add unnecessary padding to your comments and detract from your main point. Simply say what you have to say. Rather than "It is worth mentioning that we are on track to meet the deadline," say, "We are on track to meet the deadline." Similarly, replace "Given the fact that the project is behind schedule" with the simpler "Because the project is behind schedule."

"False eloquence is exaggeration; true eloquence is emphasis."

— William R. Alger, unitarian minister and abolitionist

Learn the local lingo, but don't use it excessively

Every organization has its own language—the acronyms, jargon and insider terms that the organization favors. This "local language" acts as a shorthand, helping teams communicate quickly and efficiently. Unfortunately, no one hands you a glossary on day one, so you have to pick up the lingo gradually. Your increasing familiarity and comfort with it signal that you've integrated into the culture.

However, there's a fine line between learning the lingo and overusing it. While it's important to understand and use this specialized language within your organization, relying on it too heavily can alienate those outside your immediate circle. Acronyms, buzzwords and industry-specific jargon can quickly take over your vocabulary, making your communication confusing to anyone unfamiliar with these terms, such as new colleagues, board members, clients or vendors.

The key is balance. Learn the specialized vocabulary of your workplace and industry to fit in and work more efficiently, but always be mindful of when and how you use it. Consider your audience: reserve the internal shorthand for speaking with colleagues who understand it, and switch to plain, universally understandable language when communicating with those who may be unfamiliar with your organization's distinct vocabulary.

Be conscious of using filler sounds like "um" and "uh"

Nothing is more fatal to your credibility than frequently inserting filler sounds like "um" and "uh" during conversations. These fillers are distracting and make you appear less articulate and knowledgeable. The more often they occur, the harder it becomes for listeners to focus on the substance of your insights. It's important to work on eliminating them from your conversation.

The first step is recognizing that it's a problem. Ideally, you'll notice it yourself, but often someone else may bring it to your attention. If that happens, don't get defensive—recognize that it likely took them some courage to point it out, and they probably did so with good intentions. Treat their feedback as a helpful tool for improvement.

Once you're aware of the issue, start listening to yourself as you speak. You might catch some of the fillers, but it's likely that many will slip by unnoticed. To help with this, consider enlisting a trusted colleague or friend to observe your speech patterns and note when and where the fillers appear most frequently. Identifying these patterns will help you focus on reducing their usage over time.

Ridding yourself of this habit requires thinking more carefully before you speak and slowing down the pace of your delivery. This gives you more control over your speech. Sometimes the use of filler sounds comes from stalling as you try to find your place in written notes or materials. Before such a speaking occasion, review your main talking points or even practice making your remarks. At the meeting, maintain eye contact with your audience. When you're more focused on the people you're speaking to, the fillers tend to fade away.

Make your conversation memorable through stories and comparisons

Stories and analogies are powerful tools that make abstract concepts more relatable. You can make your ideas stick with your audience by weaving narratives into your conversations. Effective storytelling helps drive your message home. When discussing data, use analogies to connect the numbers to real-life scenarios, making the information more engaging and easier to understand.

Become an effective storyteller

Storytelling isn't just for bedtime; it's a powerful tool that can elevate the way you communicate in the workplace. Often, technical explanations or data-heavy presentations fall flat because they lack emotional impact or a human element to make the information stick. This is what storytelling provides. Weaving a narrative or using a relatable analogy can make your material more memorable and can make complex concepts easier to grasp. In a business context, stories can be used to clarify strategy, convey company values, justify decisions or simply to make a message resonate. A well-crafted story has the power to shift perspectives and inspire action.

There are several steps involved in harnessing the power of storytelling:

- **Understand the elements of a great story:** Focus on the core components of a story: a clear beginning, middle and end, a challenge or conflict that needs resolution, and relatable characters or situations. These elements give a story structure and emotional focus. While details can make a story vivid, be careful not to overwhelm your audience with too much information. Keep your narrative concise and focused on the key points so your message lands effectively.

- **Incorporate emotion and authenticity:** Stories are not just about conveying facts; they're about connecting with your audience on an emotional level. Don't be afraid to add a touch of humor, surprise or even vulnerability to your storytelling. A well-timed joke or a heartfelt moment can make your message more relatable and compelling. The key is to stay authentic—forced humor or exaggerated emotions can come across as insincere.

- **Practice your delivery:** Like any other skill, storytelling improves with practice. Start by incorporating small stories into one-on-one conversations, team meetings and presentations. Observe how your audience responds—do they lean in and appear involved? Do they recall your points more easily when framed as a story? Use this feedback to refine your approach and hone your ability to tell stories that captivate, persuade and inspire.

- **Build a story library:** Start collecting a set of stories that you can draw from whenever you need to illustrate a point or highlight a lesson. These stories don't have to be based on your own personal experiences—although they can be—they can be drawn from a happening within the industry or current or historical events. You can also share stories that others have shared with you. The goal is to find narratives that resonate with your audience and reinforce the message you want to convey. Having a variety of stories at your disposal means you will be more likely to have the right one for the situation.

While storytelling can be a powerful communication tool, it's not appropriate for every situation. Stories work best in presentations, speeches or strategic conversations where there's time to delve into a narrative. In quick updates or highly technical discussions, storytelling can be more of a distraction than a benefit. Pick the moments when your story adds value; avoid moments when they could be seen as wasting time or veering off track.

An example of storytelling: misselling and the green cabbage

Discussions of misselling (deliberate misrepresentation of a product or service or pitching the product or service at an inappropriate demographic) in a professional setting can often be detached and clinical, with the conversation dominated by talk of failed controls, misaligned incentives and bad tone at the top. In such discussions, it's easy to describe the dangers of tying aggressive sales targets to high-commission pay structures, but it's far harder to explain that subtler, often hidden, incentives can be even more damaging.

That's where storytelling makes all the difference.

Take the case of an insurance company that was rocked by a major misselling scandal. After a thorough investigation, the company discovered that the unethical behavior wasn't driven by the usual suspects like commission structures or unrealistic sales targets. Instead, the root cause was something as absurd as a green cabbage.

A manager at the company had introduced a peculiar form of negative reinforcement: he would place a cabbage on the desk of the salesperson who underperformed the most against their targets. The cabbage became a visible symbol of failure, something no one wanted to be associated with. To avoid being labeled the "cabbage person," salespeople started cutting corners and misselling insurance policies. The fear of public humiliation represented by a simple vegetable became a powerful motivator, pushing employees to achieve their targets at the expense of ethical behavior.

This story works on several levels. The image of a cabbage on a desk is easy to visualize and evokes a clear sense of the pressure these employees faced. Most people can relate to the fear of being publicly singled out as a failure. And because it's such an unusual scenario, it sticks with you—you don't often hear about cabbages in a business context, making the story powerful and memorable. Most importantly, it drives home the key point: even seemingly trivial incentives can lead to significant and unintended consequences.

That's the true power of a good story: it makes abstract concepts concrete, relatable and unforgettable.

Make data relatable in conversations

When discussing data in conversations, go beyond raw numbers by making them resonate on a human level. Don't just state figures; weave them into a narrative that connects with people's experiences and emotions. There are many approaches:

- **Emphasize the effect:** Highlight the direct effect of the data in ways that matter to your audience. Instead of saying, "We reduced our energy consumption by 25%," reframe it: "Our 25% reduction means we're saving enough energy each year to power hundreds of homes. It's making a real difference in our community's carbon footprint." This makes the data more tangible and relevant, connecting numbers to real-world benefits.

- **Humanize the numbers:** Shift the focus from the data itself to the people behind it or affected by it. Instead of a dry statement like "Employee training programs have expanded by 40%," use "Our 40% increase in employee training programs means more team members are gaining the skills they need to grow in their roles and feel more confident every day." Framing data in terms of personal impact is more engaging and relatable.

- **Use familiar comparisons:** Help your audience grasp large or abstract numbers by relating them to something familiar. Instead of saying, "The new warehouse covers 50,000 square meters," make it more visual with "Our new warehouse is almost the size of 10 football fields." Or when discussing energy use, clarify "900 kilowatt-hours" by adding "That's enough to power an average US home for a month." These comparisons make the data easier to understand and more memorable.

- **Simplify data with intuitive fractions:** Transform percentages into simpler fractions or relatable proportions to make the information more digestible. Instead of saying, "15% of our clients prefer this service," you might say, "About one in seven clients choose this option." For complex concepts like confidence levels, break them down into everyday terms: rather than just stating a "95% confidence level," explain it: "In 1 out of every 20 scenarios, the outcome might differ from our prediction." For higher levels, like 99.9%, you might add, "That's just 1 in 1,000 cases falling outside the expected range."

Build trust through self-awareness and balanced dialogue

Self-awareness is crucial for keeping conversations from being self-focused or one-sided. It includes understanding when to use "we" rather than "I" to foster inclusivity and being careful not to highlight hierarchy unnecessarily. It means restraining yourself so as not to dominate the conversation and thinking twice before rephrasing someone else's thoughts, which can come off as overbearing.

Know when to use "we" instead of "I"

One of the most common communication pitfalls for business professionals is overusing the word "I." A former colleague once referred to this as "I-itis"—the habit of starting every sentence with "I have done...," "I think..." or "I would suggest..." While it's natural to emphasize your personal contributions, it's important to recognize the broader context of your work, especially in team-driven environments:

- **Use "we" as your standard:** In business, success usually depends on collective experience and capabilities, not solely on the merits of one individual. While your expertise is part of that success, it's rarely the whole story. Using "we" emphasizes that your success is part of a larger team effort. Phrases like "We think..." or "We've done..." signal you're working collaboratively, reducing the risk of appearing self-serving or egotistical. They also highlight the fact that the work is a collective effort and that clients or other stakeholders are receiving the benefit of an entire team's input, not just your individual perspective.

- **Correct "I" with "we" when necessary:** If you catch yourself using "I" inappropriately, quickly rephrase it to something like, "I meant to say that we, as a team, have been working on this approach" or if that accentuates the slip too much, simply switch back to "we" going forward.

- **Use "I" when personal opinions are warranted:** There are moments when using "I" is not only appropriate, but preferable to using "we." When a colleague or client seeks your specific perspective, or when you are volunteering an opinion that may not be reflective of the team overall, then it's best to use "I." Express your opinion thoughtfully. For example, preface your response with, "There may be differing views within the team, but if you're asking for my personal take..." This approach clarifies that your response reflects your own thinking only.

Overusing "I" also risks creating a dependency on you as the sole point of contact. If senior executives or clients perceive you as the main or only driver of insights and actions, they'll expect you to be involved in every decision, which can quickly overload your schedule and prevent your team from building independent relationships and stature. This stunts team growth and limits their ownership of important work, creating a lose-lose situation for everyone. Using "we" empowers your team, builds trust and gives confidence in the continuity and reliability of the work, with or without you.

Be mindful of accentuating hierarchy

Many organizations promote the idea that they are nonhierarchical, saying things like "Everyone can be a leader" or "We operate with a flat structure." While these ideals are admirable and aim to motivate everyone, the truth is hierarchy exists almost everywhere, and the business world is famously hierarchical, for all its attempts not to be. That's not to say hierarchy is inherently bad—it provides structure, defines responsibilities and enables accountability. Problems arise, however, when small, repeated actions reinforce hierarchy in ways that stifle engagement of more junior colleagues or perpetuate discrimination—for example, in the form of gender bias. Small practices can help:

- **List names in alphabetical order, not by seniority:** A common way hierarchy gets subtly reinforced is by listing contributors to a group report or recipients of a group email in order of seniority, or worse, listing men's names before women's, even when they have the same level of seniority. An easy fix is to list names alphabetically, which sends a subtle yet powerful message that you value everyone equally.

- **Avoid always asking the most senior person to speak first:** Another way hierarchy creeps into everyday interactions is during meetings when asking for opinions. Starting with the most senior person can unintentionally signal that their view matters more or that others should align with it. Instead, try asking junior team members to speak first. This encourages more candid input and allows them to share their perspectives without the influence of senior colleagues. If it is fitting for senior participants to speak first—such as when others need to understand their position or guidance—the senior participants can be encouraged in advance to invite input. For example, a senior leader might say, "Here's my perspective, but I'd like to hear from everyone else, especially if you see it differently. If you do see it differently, I'm also interested in why."

- **Be mindful of hierarchy when allocating tasks:** The ways tasks are allocated can show a bias to hierarchy: the most challenging or interesting tasks consistently get given to senior team members while more junior staff are left with routine busywork. This can be demotivating and limit the development of your team. Instead, distribute opportunities more evenly, so junior members have the chance to take on stretch assignments that foster growth.

Avoid dominating the discussion

As mentioned in the section on meetings, it's not good to let anyone monopolize too much speaking time. It's frustrating, stifles diverse input and causes others to disengage. When one person dominates, others hesitate to jump in, and valuable insights may be lost. Knowing how irritating and potentially damaging it is when others engage in this behavior, endeavor not to engage in it yourself.

Self-awareness is key. Be mindful of how much airtime you're taking up. If you've been speaking for several minutes without interruption, pause and ask yourself, "Am I giving others a chance to contribute?" Better yet, invite others to share their thoughts directly: "I've been talking for a while; does anyone else want to weigh in?" This simple gesture fosters a more inclusive conversation.

If you're leading the meeting, it's even more important to model this behavior. Guide the discussion, but don't dominate it. Encourage balanced dialogue by asking open-ended questions and then deliberately stepping back. Follow the advice in the section in Part 2 on managing interpersonal dynamics in meetings to keep participation balanced in a healthy way.

> "No man would listen to you if he didn't know it was his turn next."
>
> — E. W. Howe, novelist and magazine editor

Be careful clarifying someone else's comments in public

You may have had this experience: you're in a meeting where a colleague's point seems to fall flat, and you feel the urge to step in to clarify. But you need to restrain yourself. While your intention might be to help move the conversation forward, phrases like "I think what Mark is trying to say is…" can easily come off as condescending or presumptuous. You risk undermining your colleague or appearing as though you're positioning yourself as the more insightful speaker:

- **Pause before intervening:** Before jumping in to rephrase or clarify someone else's point, ask yourself whether it's truly necessary. Are people genuinely confused? If there isn't an immediate need for clarification, give your colleague space to finish their thought. Often, people just need time to fully explain themselves, and cutting them off may disrupt their flow and undermine their confidence.

- **Frame your input as an addition, not a correction:** If you do feel the need to clarify or build on a colleague's point, use phrases that highlight collaboration rather than correction. For example, say, "To add to what Mark is saying…" or "Building on Mark's point…" This approach signals that you are contributing to the conversation without implying that Mark's original point was unclear or incomplete. It shifts the focus from fixing the message to enhancing it.

- **Use clarifying questions instead of rephrasing:** Instead of rephrasing your colleague's statement, ask them to elaborate. For instance, you could ask, "Mark, could you explain how this connects to X?" or "You're making a good point—can you elaborate on that?" This way, the original speaker can clarify their message without you taking over. It avoids the suggestion that they were unclear or failed to express their thoughts well.

- **Keep gender dynamics in mind:** If you're a man and the speaker is a woman and you're tempted to clarify her point, be especially mindful of how your actions may be perceived. Using phrases like "I think what Jane's trying to say is..." can come across as a condescending assumption that she, a woman, is less knowledgeable than you, a man, are. Instead, use the approach suggested above: focus on asking questions that invite her to clarify her point directly. This approach avoids reinforcing bad gender dynamics and keeps the speaker's authority intact.

- **Correct yourself when necessary:** If you catch yourself in the act of rephrasing someone else's point unnecessarily, don't be afraid to step back and acknowledge it. You might say something like "Actually, Mark, do you want to expand on that yourself?" This shows self-awareness and demonstrates your willingness to let others share their ideas independently.

- **Check your motivation:** It's important to examine why you feel the need to clarify. Are you genuinely trying to help, or is there a part of you that's trying to appear more knowledgeable? If your motivation is to rescue the conversation to showcase your own understanding, reconsider whether this intervention is truly helpful. If you find yourself frequently stepping in to translate points, it could signal a habit of seeking the spotlight rather than fostering productive discussion.

"The true spirit of conversation consists in building on another man's observation, not overturning it."

— Edward G. Bulwer-Lytton, novelist and politician

Handle conflict with confidence and clarity

Part of handling conflict is heading it off before it can begin. This is why it's advisable not to talk about polarizing, high-emotion, non-work-related topics at work—topics such as politics and religion. Nevertheless, conflicts will arise, and it's important not to ignore them. Addressing them early on, when they are still small, can prevent them from escalating. Manage conflict thoughtfully, seeking to find common ground even if it means backtracking to areas of agreement. While you should be prepared to agree to disagree at times, make sure it's not your go-to solution; aim for resolution or an agreed course of action whenever possible.

Stay off politics and religion in conversation

Politics and religion are among the most emotionally charged topics that can come up in conversation. While these subjects are deeply important to many, they rarely belong in professional settings, where the focus is on fostering collaboration, productivity and inclusivity.

> "It's rude to talk about religion. You never know who you're gonna offend."
>
> — Ed Bloom in *Big Fish* (2003)

Engaging in political or religious discussions at work can quickly lead to discomfort, division and even conflict:

- **Recognize the distinction between geopolitics and politics:** There's an important difference between discussing geopolitics—such as international policies, global regulations or market impacts—and engaging in political debates about specific parties, politicians or personal ideologies. While conversations about global issues or regulatory changes are often relevant to business, avoid turning these into debates over political beliefs because this can quickly create conflict or discomfort.

- **Restrain yourself from engaging:** Even if you feel strongly about a political or religious issue, recognize when and where it's appropriate to discuss these topics. In a work context, exercise restraint. Be aware that discussing current affairs or news of the day can unintentionally veer into political or religious territory. If a colleague makes a statement that sparks a political debate, resist the urge to engage or argue.

- **Redirect conversations when politics or religion arise:** If politics or religion surface during a team meeting, tactfully steer the conversation back to work-related matters. For example, if a political comment is made, you might say, "I understand this is an important issue, but let's focus on what we need to accomplish today." This approach acknowledges the significance of the topic without encouraging further discussion.

- **Offer neutral, inclusive alternatives:** To build rapport while keeping discussions neutral, consider focusing on current events related to industry trends, professional development or lighter subjects like travel, food or shared hobbies. These topics encourage connection without the emotional weight that can create tension. But when suggesting a switch in topics avoid trivializing the initial subject matter.

Don't ignore major problems

In many workplaces, glaring issues—often called the "800 lb. gorillas"—are left unaddressed. Problems such as toxic dynamics, process inefficiencies or harmful policies are obvious to everyone, but no one brings them up. Fear of rocking the boat, being labeled a troublemaker or appearing uncooperative can prevent people from addressing these uncomfortable realities. Yet ignoring these problems solves nothing and often makes them worse. To foster a healthy workplace, you need to be willing to acknowledge and confront these issues directly with care:

- **Recognize the effect of staying silent:** When everyone is aware of a problem but no one speaks up, it creates a culture of avoidance. However, staying silent signals that the status quo is acceptable, even when it's clearly not, and the longer an issue is ignored, the harder it becomes to fix. Recognizing that silence often equates to complicity is the first step toward driving positive change.

- **Choose the right moment and offer solutions:** Once you have decided to tackle one of these 800 lb. gorillas, timing and approach matter. Don't bring the issue up at the height of a tense negotiation or the last stages of a project. Instead, wait for a relatively tranquil period. Consider how to frame the conversation constructively. For instance, if a manager's leadership style is causing tension, instead of outright criticism, suggest specific ways communication or collaboration could improve. Avoid the appearance of simply complaining. Instead, show that you've thought about the issue and have ideas for improvement. Saying, "I see this as a problem, and here's how we might fix it" is far more effective than simply pointing out what's wrong.

> "If nothing changes, nothing changes."
> — Nicholas Donofrio, author and former IBM executive vice president

- **Be prepared to face resistance, but lead with courage:** Speaking up, especially when no one else has, can be uncomfortable. You might face resistance, particularly if the issue involves senior leaders or is deeply ingrained in the organization. Calling out major issues is a hallmark of true leadership, however. It demonstrates accountability and ownership and shows you care about the organization's long-term success. Courageous conversations, while uncomfortable in the short term, often lead to healthier and more effective workplaces.
- **Take responsibility for the outcome:** After offering solutions, be involved in the resolution. This could mean leading discussions and taking on a specific role in implementing a solution. Staying engaged and taking responsibility for next steps makes your commitment to progress clear.

In a leadership role, aim for impartiality when managing conflict

When conflict arises, handle it with fairness, diplomacy and sensitivity. You have a responsibility to steer the discussion constructively:

- **Stay neutral and focused on the bigger picture:** You should manage conflict fairly. Even if you're in sympathy with one side, attempt to maintain neutrality. Focus on the broader goals of the meeting or project. For example, if the conflict centers on how to present progress so far on a project, frame the discussion in terms of the ultimate objective—project completion. You might say, "Our main goal here is to deliver this project on time. Let's consider what our next steps toward that goal are and see if that will give us some clarity on how to present on progress so far." While you may prefer one time frame, avoid steering the conversation too directly toward your preferred outcome.
- **Encourage each side to voice their perspective:** Provide each person or side the chance to explain their position without being interrupted. Ask clarifying questions that allow each side to articulate their concerns and actively listen to what they say. For example, "It sounds like there's a concern about resources being stretched. Can you elaborate on how you see this affecting the timeline?" Be sure to give equal weight to both sides to maintain neutrality and promote productive dialogue.
- **Propose structured solutions:** Once both sides have shared their views, guide the conversation toward solutions. Without taking a side, offer structured proposals that reflect the concerns of both parties. For example, "We've heard that the timeline is a concern and that resources are tight. Could we explore relaxing some deadlines to free up time? And are there any budget reallocations we can look at to address the resource problem?" Proposing middle-ground solutions shows you're invested in resolving the issue, not just managing the discussion.
- **Reframe the conflict:** Sometimes conflicts escalate because participants feel personally attacked. In those situations, redirect the conversation to focus on the issue rather than the individuals. If someone accuses someone else of not being supportive of the team, try saying, "It sounds like there's a concern about how team support is structured. How can we improve communication around team needs?" This moves the conversation away from blame and toward problem solving.
- **Know when to call for compromise:** If the conflict seems unresolvable, it's important to push the conversation toward compromise. Reiterate that complete agreement isn't always necessary, but finding a workable solution is. For example, "It seems like we may not all

agree on the exact approach, but can we find a short-term plan that provides a way forward?" Encourage both parties to find areas of flexibility without forcing a single right answer.

After the meeting or conversation, follow up with both sides to be sure that the agreed-upon solution is implemented and no lingering resentment remains. A simple check-in—"just wanted to see how everyone is feeling after our discussion"—can go a long way in maintaining trust and a sense of collaboration. If any concerns persist, be ready to address them before they grow into larger issues.

> "You never really understand a person until you consider things from his point of view."
>
> — Harper Lee, writer

If there's complete misalignment, walk backwards until there isn't

When a group is deeply divided, the natural instinct is often for both parties to keep reiterating their point of view, hoping that persistence will eventually lead to agreement. However, this approach typically results in frustration and further entrenchment, not progress. A senior colleague of mine had a more effective strategy: "walk backwards" in the conversation until you find a point where common ground still exists. From there, you can rebuild the discussion in a more collaborative and productive manner:

- **Recognize shared objectives:** That people are in the room together suggests that there is some commonality—otherwise, there would be no discussion at all. Start by identifying this shared interest or goal. For example, if two teams are at an impasse over strategy, you might take the conversation back to a fundamental goal like improving business performance or better serving customers. Acknowledging this shared objective creates a collaborative mindset and reduces tension, setting the stage for more productive dialogue.

- **Identify areas of agreement:** After recognizing the shared goal, look for specific areas of agreement. These might be values or priorities that both sides hold, even if they've diverged on the methods to achieve them. For instance, both teams might agree that increasing customer satisfaction is a priority but differ on the approach. Identifying areas of alignment eases some of the emotional strain and makes moving forward together seem more possible.

- **Rebuild the conversation from a point of alignment:** Once you've found common ground, use it as the foundation for progress together. Rebuild the conversation incrementally, step by step, shifting the focus from disagreement to collaboration. For example, if everyone agrees on the importance of customer satisfaction, you can begin exploring tactical steps to achieve that goal that both parties can agree on. The goal is to rebuild the discussion based on mutual trust and shared interests before delving into the more complex or contentious issues.

- **Agree on how to address points of disagreement:** Not every issue can or should be resolved immediately, but after realigning on shared goals and agreed actions, create a plan for addressing the remaining points of contention. This could involve deciding which team's strategy to trial first, agreeing to test both ideas or escalating the issue to senior leadership for a final decision. For example, two managers might disagree on how to structure a project team, but after realigning on a shared project goal, they could agree to try one approach for a set period before reassessing.

Walking backwards to find common ground encourages active listening and empathy. Focusing on what both parties value rather than what they oppose creates an environment where participants are more likely to hear each other out. This promotes a sense of collaboration and reduces defensiveness.

> "Cooperation isn't the absence of conflict but a means of managing conflict."
>
> — Deborah Tannen, professor of linguistics

Be prepared to agree to disagree, just not all the time

In professional settings, smart, reasonable people can reach agreement on an issue through open dialogue, sharing perspectives and problem solving. However, there are moments when no amount of debate, meetings or persuasion will bridge the gap between differing viewpoints—and that's okay. Agreeing to disagree can be a mature and acceptable outcome. The key is knowing when and how to do this gracefully and to agree on a way forward:

- **Recognize when to agree to disagree:** When it becomes clear that no consensus can be reached despite reasonable efforts, continuing the debate is unproductive. Forcing alignment sows the seeds of future problems and may result ultimately in failure. Focus on maintaining mutual respect and professionalism. If you're one of the parties in the conflict, avoid giving the impression that you're disappointed or frustrated because the other party didn't "get it." (If you're more senior, avoid giving the impression that you're disappointed in both parties.) Calmly acknowledge the difference in perspectives without making it personal. For instance, you might say, "I see we have different views on this/I see there are different views on this, and that's fine. Let's focus on what we do next."

- **Value the discussion, even if no consensus is reached:** Agreeing to disagree doesn't mean the discussion was a failure. Engaging with different perspectives can lead to greater understanding and deeper insights. Sometimes the debate itself can clarify each party's thinking and spark new ideas, even if alignment wasn't achieved. For instance, while two colleagues may disagree on a marketing strategy, the conversation might reveal ways to incorporate elements from both ideas into future campaigns.

- **Decide on next steps:** After agreeing to disagree on the point of contention, the parties need to decide what comes next. If the irreconcilable point is relatively minor, an arbitrary decision can be taken that lets work proceed. For example, if two managers disagree over team structure, one structure can be arbitrarily picked, with the understanding that adjustments can be made later if needed. This allows the team to continue working without wasting time or energy.

If the issue is more substantive and neither party can agree to the other's plan, decide how to escalate the matter to senior colleagues collaboratively. This option prevents a stalemate and moves the issue forward, but it should be used sparingly—frequent escalation can give the impression that you're obstructive or unable to resolve differences independently.

* * * * *

Mastering advanced conversational techniques allows you to navigate any professional interaction with confidence and clarity. By honing your ability to use and recognize nonverbal cues and by sharpening your active listening and storytelling skills, you are equipping yourself to build strong, trust-based relationships. Next we will explore fine-tuning your communication in the areas of staying informed, communicating in an inclusive and respectful manner and dealing with conversational danger zones—essential skills for thriving in today's diverse and interconnected workplace.

PART  Fine-Tuning Your Communication

Part 4 covers broadening your knowledge for richer discussions, increasing your conversational sensitivity and dealing with conversational danger zones.

In Part 4

- Stay informed to contribute meaningfully to discussions.
- Broaden your horizons—and bring that knowledge into conversations.
- Communicate inclusively, respecting cultural differences.
- Use gender-neutral and nondiscriminatory language.
- Handle conversational danger zones with care and professionalism.

Stay informed to contribute meaningfully to discussions

Staying informed and continually growing your knowledge base makes your participation in (and leadership of) discussions richer and more meaningful. When you are aware of current news and business trends, you can contribute confidently to conversations on all levels, from casual office chatter to strategic meetings. Actively seek opportunities to deepen your understanding, share insights with others and embrace new learning experiences.

Keep current on news and business

Talking about what's happening in the world demonstrates your interest and involvement in external events and the issues shaping the global landscape. Current events are often the foundation for casual business interactions. It's common for someone to start a meeting by asking, "Did you see the news this morning about [topic]?" This is usually a top news item, not something obscure. If you stay on top of major stories, you'll be able to respond with a yes and engage with the topic. If you know the person you're meeting has a particular interest, you might even be the one to bring it up, using it as a bridge to a deeper conversation. You don't need to be an expert on every topic, but cultivating an interest in a broad array will make it possible for you to contribute more meaningfully to many discussions.

Develop a routine for keeping up with current affairs, being sure to include such topics as geopolitics, national news, industry updates and trends relevant to your profession. Consult a variety of media sources to get a well-rounded view. Each news outlet has its own biases, so following different sources will help you get a more balanced perspective. International sources like the BBC, *Financial Times* or *The Economist* offer a more global perspective than US news outlets and are generally more neutral. If your role requires deep industry knowledge, subscribe to specialized publications in your field—consider it a valuable investment in your professional growth.

If you invest in a subscription to a print version of a news source such as *The Wall Street Journal* or the *Financial Times*, it's also worthwhile to bring it along to meetings. It can be an effective and memorable prop for an opening question or remark relating to the topic of the meeting—a prompt to spark discussion.

Some business writers advise staying up to date on major sports as well. In the US, especially, it's common for business conversations to involve references to the latest golf tournament, football game or basketball playoffs. If you can and want to engage, go for it. But while discussing sports is part of business culture, trying to feign interest in sports you don't follow is unlikely to succeed. It's hard enough to keep up with a sport you like, let alone several you don't. If you're not interested in a particular sport or any sports, be honest about it. For example, if someone asks about a recent game, you can say, "I don't follow football, but I'm more into [another hobby or sport]." This response is authentic, and people will appreciate your honesty. Not everyone is a sports enthusiast, and it's perfectly acceptable to steer the conversation toward shared interests.

Keep abreast of the topics that constitute office small talk

The broader social and cultural milieu forms the bedrock of office small talk. Having a sense of what's going on in popular culture—whether it's movies, TV shows or social media—can help you connect with colleagues on a more personal level. Even if popular culture isn't your main area of interest, keeping up with it can open doors to light, engaging conversations that build rapport. (Why, you may ask, am I suggesting that you make an effort with pop culture even if it isn't your interest when I didn't make that suggestion for sports? My answer is that pop culture is an even bigger part of our collective lives. For that reason, it's also easier stay casually aware of pop culture than it is to stay abreast of sports—pop culture is covered by media everywhere.)

Start with TV shows and movies. Learn what's been released recently and have a few recommendations ready. People appreciate hearing about new shows or films to add to their watchlists, and talking about something you've seen makes for an easy, natural conversation. Similarly, have some book recommendations handy. Almost everyone enjoys adding new reads to their booklist, and a shared discussion about a popular book can be a great way to bond. However, be authentic—if you mention a show, movie or book, make sure you've watched or read it. People can usually tell if you're bluffing.

Feel confident in your personal preferences. You don't need to be into the latest highbrow or trendy shows to engage in these conversations. Don't shy away from bringing up genres or topics that genuinely interest you, whether it's nature documentaries, obscure indie films or classic literature. Sharing what you're passionate about will resonate more than trying to fit into someone else's mold. You might be surprised at how many colleagues or clients share your interests.

Depending on your personal interests, keeping somewhat up to date on celebrity news or trending cultural topics can be helpful. You don't need to know who Timothée Chalamet, Selena Gomez or Tom Holland are dating, but having a general awareness of popular cultural figures can help you feel more engaged when others bring them up. If you're unsure about a trend or topic, don't hesitate to ask someone, especially younger colleagues or family members. While they might tease you for being out of the loop, they'll likely appreciate your interest and effort to stay tuned in.

Broaden your horizons—and bring that knowledge into conversations

One of the most powerful ways to grow, both personally and professionally, is to constantly seek out new challenges. When you encounter new tasks or projects, don't just skim the surface. Dive deep to gain an understanding of the underlying issues. Even if you have strong expertise in one area, building knowledge across a range of topics makes you more versatile, interesting and valuable. The key is to push yourself beyond your comfort zone, continually tackling roles or projects where you initially feel out of your depth.

Learn from work interactions

Not all learning opportunities will be daunting. Meetings with colleagues or clients often present chances to absorb new perspectives, but you need to consciously transform these moments into lasting knowledge. Pay attention, reflect on what you are hearing and find ways to share what you've learned in your own voice:

- **Listen, take notes and do follow-up research:** Every meeting, conversation or presentation offers the possibility of new insights. Listen attentively and note both the content and how ideas are being communicated and framed. Take notes on how people are approaching the subject, their thought processes and the underlying issues. If you encounter something unfamiliar or a concept that piques your interest, make a point to follow up with further research. For example, if someone mentions a marketing strategy that's unfamiliar, make a note of it so you can explore it in depth later.

- **Debrief and reflect on what you've learned:** Afterward, take the time to review your notes, reflect on the experience and, if necessary, debrief with a colleague or mentor who attended the same meeting. Compare notes with a teammate to clarify key points and to be sure neither of you overlooked anything significant. This follow-up process will strengthen your understanding and surface different interpretations or reveal deeper layers of the discussion that you hadn't initially noticed or considered.

- **Contribute meaningfully to future discussions in your own words:** When opportunities arise, use what you've learned to contribute meaningfully to conversations and meetings. Even if you're still working through the material, sharing your evolving thoughts signals that you're engaged and interested in growing. But don't simply parrot back what you heard; put your thoughts into your own words.

"A single conversation across the table with a wise man is better than ten years mere study of books."

— Henry Wadsworth Longfellow, poet and educator

Step boldly out of your comfort zone

Some of the most profound work experiences come from challenging yourself with roles or projects that stretch your current capabilities. That initial discomfort—wondering if you're in over your head—is often the precursor to real growth. These challenges exercise your capacity to learn and offer the opportunity to develop new skills and insights:

- **Seek roles outside your expertise:** For example, if you have a background in operations, consider volunteering for a project that requires collaboration with the finance team. Exposure to unfamiliar areas will not only broaden your skill set and prepare you for future challenges and projects, it will increase your understanding of the overall enterprise and give you insight into the problems and perspectives of people in other parts of the business.

- **Ask questions to deepen your knowledge:** Questions like "What do these acronyms actually stand for?" or "Why does this stakeholder care so much about issue X when Y seems more important?" help break down barriers and clarify the essentials. Go deeper by asking, "What's the underlying driver of this decision?" or "How does this process fit into the bigger picture?" These questions can help others understand important information and may reveal gaps in understanding or logic that they were unaware of or were hesitant to express.

- **Collaborate on learning frameworks:** When discussing unfamiliar projects, collaborate with colleagues or mentors to create visual frameworks that simplify complex topics. For example, you might work with your team to build a whiteboard diagram that maps out how different business functions interact. Cocreating these visual clarifies the material and helps the team collectively understand and retain the information.

Communicate inclusively, respecting cultural differences

Effective communication goes beyond clear expression; it involves being mindful of inclusivity and respect. When dealing with international colleagues or clients, you need to be aware of cultural differences in formality, communication styles and humor so you can adapt your style appropriately. In some countries, a casual approach may be welcomed, while in others, a more formal tone is necessary. If you're unsure, err on the side of caution by adopting a more formal tone initially and adjust as needed based on the responses you receive. When dealing with humor, as noted in Part 3, be mindful that what's funny in one culture may not resonate—or may even offend—in another.

Whether at home or abroad, show respect by avoiding language that's implicitly biased (for example, metaphors that are disparaging to women, older people or people with disabilities) and opting for gender-neutral terms that create a welcoming environment for everyone.

Be mindful of your idioms and metaphors

English is the international language of business, but idioms and informal expressions that are common in one English-speaking culture may not translate well to others and may be impenetrable for people who are not native speakers. Instead of saying, "Our expansion strategy is to hit the ground running in the Asian markets," which may confuse nonnative English speakers, say, "Our expansion strategy is to quickly establish our presence in the Asian markets through strategic partnerships and local marketing." This avoids a potentially confusing idiom and provides illustrative concrete details.

Similarly, using aggressive or warlike metaphors can be problematic, especially in regions that have experienced conflict. Phrases like "We'll employ a guerrilla marketing strategy that aggressively targets consumers" can be unsettling in some contexts. A better alternative is to say, "We plan to adopt an innovative marketing strategy, carefully tailored to respect and engage with local customs and consumer preferences." This phrasing removes the war imagery and highlights a thoughtful and respectful approach to entering a new market.

Use gender-neutral and nonableist language

Gender-neutral language shows respect and professionalism. Small shifts, such as replacing the exclusive use of "he" or the awkward use of "he or she" with the singular "they" can go a long way in fostering inclusivity. For instance, instead of saying, "When a client asks for a meeting, he or she should be given a prompt response," use, "When a client asks for a meeting, they should be given a prompt response." The singular "they" has been used for centuries and is now widely accepted as a gender-neutral pronoun. While most people will welcome this shift, some may push back against the singular "they," arguing that it sounds ungrammatical. If you encounter this, you can often rephrase the sentence to avoid the issue. For example, "When clients ask for a meeting, they should be given a prompt response" maintains clarity while using a plural subject, which sounds more natural to critics of the singular "they."

Another way to make your language more inclusive is by using gender-neutral job titles. Instead of saying, "The chairman will address the board," say, "The chair will address the board." This simple change avoids the assumption that certain roles are predominantly male or female, even if today some are that way.

Equally important is respecting people's pronoun preferences. If someone shares their pronouns with you—whether they're he/him, she/her, they/them or another option—use them consistently, even if they feel unfamiliar or unusual at first. Misusing or ignoring someone's pronouns can be highly hurtful, and it reflects poorly on your professionalism. You can practice using these pronouns in conversations with third parties when the person in question isn't present to help yourself grow accustomed to them. If you make a mistake, correct yourself and move forward without dwelling on it.

Language that overlooks the experiences of individuals with disabilities can inadvertently propagate attitudes that discriminate in favor of able-bodied people (ableism). While such phrases are often used without ill intent, they can reinforce negative stereotypes and promote exclusion. Choosing your words carefully allows you to express your thoughts in a way that is respectful and inclusive of all individuals.

One of the most effective ways to do this is through people-first language, which emphasizes the person rather than the disability. For example, saying "colleagues with dyslexia" is more respectful and humanizing than "dyslexic colleagues" or "dyslexics."

You can also replace ableist phrases with alternatives that respect everyone's experiences. For example, instead of saying, "We've identified a blind spot in our strategy," you can say, "We've identified an overlooked area in our strategy." Similarly, rather than describing inconsistent leadership as "schizophrenic," a better, neutral alternative is to say, "Our leadership lacks consistency, oscillating between strategies."

Other common phrases, like "The department is finally standing on its own two feet" or "Our team is tone-deaf in its messaging," can easily be replaced with more inclusive language. You can say, "The department is becoming independent and self-sufficient" or "Our team is insensitive in its messaging." These alternatives preserve the original meaning without relying on metaphors linked to disabilities.

Handle conversational danger zones with care and professionalism

Good workplace relations depend on awareness of and sensitivity to personal boundaries. A personal compliment that one person thinks of as polite or gallant may be seen by another as inappropriate. Similarly, the permissibility of colorful language (cursing, expletives, swear words) varies greatly from workplace to workplace. Finally, almost all workplaces have one or two abrasive colleagues. This section offers some strategies for dealing with them.

Think before complimenting someone's appearance

We live in a work environment in which it is necessary to be hyperaware of how our words might be perceived. The last thing any of us want is to make a colleague feel uncomfortable or disrespected.

However, it's still possible to offer a genuine, kind comment about someone's appearance—like complimenting a new tie, suit or haircut—without crossing any lines, so long as you keep in mind the following:

- **Assess how well you know the person:** Consider your relationship and how well you know their comfort level. How have they reacted to other personal remarks, either from you or another person? Do they themselves offer compliments to others? Bear in mind that in some cultures, compliments on appearance are common and widely accepted, while in others, they are seen as intrusive or overly personal. If the person you wish to compliment seems comfortable with personal remarks, has offered compliments to others, and if you have a solid, respectful relationship with them, then saying, "Hey, you look great today" can be a friendly gesture. But if there's the least chance that your compliment could be taken amiss, don't offer it.

- **Focus on neutral observations:** When giving compliments, keep them brief and focus on something neutral, like clothing or a new hairstyle, rather than personal attributes. Comments such as "That's a sharp tie" or "Your haircut looks great" are generally safer than remarks about, for example, how physically fit a person has become or about changes in their weight, which could be misinterpreted as objectifying or too familiar.

- **Consider context and delivery:** How and when you deliver a compliment is just as important as what you say. Making a casual comment in passing or before a meeting, similar to how you'd discuss the weather or a recent event, is more appropriate than pulling someone aside to say the same thing.

Remember, in all your work interactions, you want to be contributing to a positive and supportive environment, and you don't want to make others uncomfortable. A compliment is acceptable if it contributes to the former, but not if it results in the latter.

Use swear words sparingly, if at all

> "Excuse me? You did just start this conversation off by saying crap, didn't you?"
>
> — Jonathan Hemlock in *The Eiger Sanction* (1975)

Swearing in the workplace can be a touchy subject, but used sparingly and in the right context, it can have a place. It's not about unleashing a tirade of expletives or using harsh language to belittle anyone—that's never acceptable. But a well-placed swear word can sometimes add emphasis or express frustration in a way that nothing else quite can. The key is to use it thoughtfully and selectively, and—as always—to keep the workplace culture in mind:

- **Gauge the context and audience:** Context is crucial when it comes to swearing at work. Avoid using strong language in formal settings, in front of clients or in any situation where it could be perceived as offensive or inappropriate. If you're among close colleagues who know you well and understand your intent, a mild expletive might add some color to the conversation without crossing any lines. For example, when venting frustration over a particularly baffling situation, saying, "I was completely pissed off when the whole thing went sideways" might convey emotion and authenticity in a relatable way, but it still could be viewed as vulgar by a close colleague. Always read the room—if you're unsure about the audience's comfort level, it's safer to hold back.

- **Use swear words sparingly:** Overusing swear words dilutes their effect and can come off as unprofessional. Reserve your strong language for truly frustrating situations ("That fricking delay set us back weeks!"); don't make it a habitual part of your language. The occasional use of a well-chosen expletive can humanize you, showing that you're as subject to frustration as the next person and not a rigidly self-controlled corporate automaton.

- **Opt for pseudo swear words over their more vulgar alternatives:** You'll note that in the previous bullet point, I used "fricking" rather than the well-known four-letter "f bomb," which is a little too hot for this instructional book. You can do similar in the workplace: "dang" is a more mild-mannered version of "damn" and "heck" is a tamer version of "hell." One colleague of mine recalls a workmate who used "sugar" as a substitute for the four-letter swear word starting with "s." Similarly, the British expression "bloody" can convey frustration or emphasis without straying into inappropriate territory. ("This bloody project is driving me up the wall!") These substitutes still express your feelings but are less likely to make others uncomfortable.

How permissible swearing is will vary from workplace to workplace. Remember that various English-speaking regions and subregions can have sensitivities regarding words that aren't so problematic in other locations and that people of different ages will have different tolerances for different words. Bearing in mind the importance of fostering a workplace in which everyone feels comfortable, it's best to be extremely sparing in your use of swear words.

Manage and limit your interactions with sharp-elbowed colleagues

Navigating office politics can feel like maneuvering through a crowded room with everyone jostling for position. In competitive workplaces, you're bound to encounter colleagues who use "sharp elbows" to push their way ahead—dominating conversations, undermining others or claiming undue credit to gain the upper hand. These tactics can turn a healthy environment into a cutthroat one, where ambition and self-interest replace collaboration. Knowing how to handle your interactions with these types of colleagues will help:

- **Spot sharp-elbowed colleagues early:** Be observant in meetings and group settings. Pay attention to who interrupts or talks over others, who always seems to take credit for team successes and who thrives on back-channel gossip. Identifying these individuals early on helps you manage your interactions thoughtfully. Once spotted, keep your communication with them brief and professional.

- **Set clear boundaries:** If you're required to work closely with sharp-elbowed colleagues, establish clear limits. Keep your interactions focused on the task at hand and avoid sharing more information than necessary. Be polite but reserved; these colleagues may seem friendly one day but use your words against you the next. By controlling the narrative and not revealing your vulnerabilities, you maintain the upper hand without engaging in their tactics.

- **Don't react impulsively:** It's tempting to push back when someone elbows you out of the way, but reacting often escalates the situation. Sharp-elbowed colleagues usually have allies who might not see their negative traits and could twist your reaction into a story about you being difficult or uncooperative. Maintain your composure and avoid feeding into their manipulative strategies.

- **Cultivate your own support network:** Align yourself with colleagues who value honesty, collaboration and respect, people you can identify in the same way you identified the sharp-elbowed colleagues: through observation in group settings. Build relationships with those who recognize genuine effort and team contributions. This mutual support network can act as a buffer for all its members against the influence of sharp-elbowed individuals and can be a counterweight against a cutthroat culture.

Above all, avoid getting caught in power struggles with sharp-elbowed colleagues. Focus on your work, deliver consistent results and stay true to your values. The good news is that karma often has a way of catching up with these people. Over time, those who rely on sharp elbows to survive tend to reveal themselves to a broader audience. While they might have protectors and enablers in the short term, those relationships are often built on shaky ground. Eventually, reputations built on manipulation and aggression crumble and integrity and genuine effort come out on top.

* * * * *

Mastering the conversational and relational nuances of social interaction in the workplace enhances your ability to adapt to diverse professional scenarios. By broadening your knowledge base, communicating inclusively and being mindful of conversational danger zones, you can navigate even the most challenging interactions with finesse. Next, we'll turn our focus to feedback and career conversations—crucial areas that will empower you to grow personally and professionally, while helping others do the same.

PART

Feedback and Career Conversations

This section delves into the art of giving and receiving feedback and using conversations to guide your career development. It emphasizes the importance of clear communication, self-awareness and proactive self-advocacy to help you grow professionally and make intentional career choices.

In Part 5

- Deliver constructive feedback with empathy and clarity.
- Actively seek feedback actively for continuous improvement.
- Use conversations to manage your career trajectory and celebrate accomplishments.
- Consciously choose your work-life balance.

Deliver constructive feedback with empathy and clarity

Some of the most important business conversations center on giving and receiving feedback and career guidance. When you are the one doing the giving, you need to be professional in your approach. First, make sure you are in a credible position from which to offer feedback so your input is valued and constructive. During the feedback conversation, use nonadversarial approaches to keep the interaction positive. When offering career advice, the guidance should aim to help the recipient make decisions that align with their own personal goals and circumstances, even if those are different from yours.

Only offer feedback if you are in a legitimate position to do so

Feedback is often described as a gift, but it's only valuable when it's rooted in knowledge and experience. Feedback on a technical report, for example, will be much more valued coming from someone with a background in that field or from someone with a lot of experience writing reports than from someone unfamiliar with the subject matter or without much writing experience. Uninformed feedback can easily lead people astray and may be perceived as grandstanding. Be honest with yourself about your suitability for the task of giving feedback in a given situation. Would it be better to let someone with deeper knowledge or better standing take the lead?

If your experience and position make you a good source of feedback, the next step is to deliver your insights in a constructive, respectful manner:

- **Frame feedback constructively, not prescriptively:** Avoid sounding prescriptive or condescending, which can cause the recipient to shut down and not take in what you're saying. Instead, frame your feedback as a collaborative suggestion. For instance, instead of saying, "You should do this differently," try, "Have you considered approaching it this way?" This approach opens the door for discussion, showing that your intent is to help rather than dictate.

- **Approach feedback outside your expertise with humility:** There will be times when you feel compelled to give feedback outside your core expertise. When you do, acknowledge your limitations and frame your input as a question or observation. For example, you might say, "I'm not an expert in this area, but I've seen X work in similar situations—might that be helpful here?" This honest admission of your lack of knowledge softens your input and shows respect for the recipient's own knowledge and judgment.

- **Avoid public corrections:** Correcting or critiquing someone in front of others can be demoralizing and humiliating. If it seems to be done to showcase your own knowledge, it can cause deep resentment. Instead of making remarks in front of others, choose a private setting where you can discuss your points respectfully. For example, instead of sending a public "reply all" email with suggested changes to a colleague's work, offer to discuss it one-on-one. This approach shows tact and consideration and will strengthen your professional relationships.

- **Be mindful of timing and delivery:** Even the most thoughtful feedback can be sensitive, so timing and delivery are crucial. Choose a stress-free moment and a private setting, such as a one-on-one conversation, rather than addressing the issue in front of the team. Begin with positive observations when possible, so that your words feel supportive rather than confrontational.

Remember, even when well-intentioned and delivered with tact, feedback may feel stinging to the recipient, especially if it relates to something that could be construed as sensitive or personal, such as the way a person presents themselves or speaks. That's where having effective feedback techniques come in, like those discussed below.

Use "the effect on me" technique

The intention of feedback is to guide and encourage growth, but it can create discomfort or defensiveness if not delivered thoughtfully. A powerful tool to help with this is the "effect on me" technique, which frames your remarks as your personal reactions rather than as speculative assumptions about how the recipient's words or actions were received or assertions that the recipient did something wrong. For example, the statement "I think the client reacted negatively when you said XYZ," is a speculative assumption: you can't know for sure how the client felt about XYZ. The "effect on me" wording used to convey that impression is more personal and concrete. You might say, "When you said XYZ, the effect on me, had it been directed at me, would have been discomfort." Grounding the conversation in your own experience removes room for debate—no one can argue with how you would have felt:

- **Keep the conversation constructive and free of accusations:** The strength of the "effect on me" technique lies in its ability to make feedback feel less like criticism and more like an observation. For example, rather than saying "You talked for 20 minutes straight and didn't let the client get a word in edgewise—that kind of behavior can lose us business," try, "I noticed you had an impressive amount information prepared for the meeting. There were several points at which, were it me you were speaking with, I would have liked to ask questions or add a comment, but you didn't provide an opportunity. The effect on me would have been to disengage from the meeting because I would have expected it to be more of a two-way dialogue."

- **Offer a pathway forward:** For feedback to be useful, it has to go beyond explaining the effect on you and provide clear guidance on how to improve. After stating how their actions would have affected you, suggest an alternative approach: "If it were me, I would have outlined your first two points and then sought a reaction. I would have let the other topics come up naturally or mentioned them when appropriate." Providing specific strategies helps turn the feedback into a growth opportunity rather than just pointing out a misstep.

Distinguish impact from intent in feedback conversations

Another effective way to provide constructive feedback is to clearly distinguish between impact and intent. This technique helps focus the conversation on the actual consequences of someone's actions, rather than getting sidetracked by their intentions:

- **Acknowledge the person's intent up front:** When someone is told their behavior negatively affected another person, their instinct is often to defend themselves with comments like "That wasn't my intent" or "I didn't mean for it to come across that way." Start by acknowledging their intent. For example, depending on the situation, you could say something like "I understand that your intention was merely to offer a strong counterpoint" or "I recognize your intent was to forcefully defend the proposal." This immediately relaxes the recipient by acknowledging their good motivations. You're not accusing them of acting maliciously. With that baseline set, the conversation can proceed constructively.

- **Shift the focus to the impact of their actions:** The crux of the feedback should focus on the impact their actions had, regardless of their intent. This is where the real issue lies. For instance, you might say, "While your intention was good, several team members commented afterward about being not being heard." Emphasizing the impact highlights the tangible consequences of their behavior, avoiding a debate over what they meant to do.

- **Guide the recipient toward self-reflection and solutions:** After clarifying the impact, encourage the individual to think about how they could handle similar situations differently in the future. Ask them to reflect by saying, "Given how things played out, what do you think you could have done differently to avoid this outcome?" This question promotes self-awareness and helps them to take ownership of their behavior. It shifts their focus to finding ways to improve.

- **Offer specific, actionable advice when appropriate:** While encouraging self-reflection is essential, there are times when direct suggestions are more helpful. You might say, "Next time, consider stopping to ask other team members' opinion before moving to the next topic" or "Take ten seconds to read the room before responding." Offering concrete advice provides the individual with clear steps they can take to avoid repeating the same mistake.

Remind the feedback recipient that while good intentions are important, how their words or actions affect people matters even more.

If asked, offer impartial career advice

Throughout my career, people have turned to me for career advice, likely because of my varied experiences across a range of work environments. This diversity of experience—spanning offices with just a few people and global companies with over 350,000 employees—has shown me that career decisions are rarely straightforward, and there's no universal answer that fits everyone. Every person's situation comes with its own set of variables, which means the best way you can help colleagues with career dilemmas, when asked, is to spur them to think about those factors. Try to keep their priorities and preferences, not your own, foremost:

- **Acknowledge your own biases and limitations:** It's easy to fall into the trap of projecting your own preferences onto someone else's decision-making process. For instance, you might be comfortable taking risks and jumping into new roles quickly, but not everyone shares that mindset. Some people might prioritize stability due to family obligations or seek to build a deeper skill set in their current position. Recognizing your experiences are yours alone helps you better support colleagues in exploring options that align with their values and circumstances.

- **Focus on impartiality in your advice:** The goal isn't to steer someone toward staying at their current job or jumping to a new opportunity. It is to provide a balanced perspective that helps your colleague weigh the pros and cons of each option. I arrived at this approach thanks to my time at McKinsey, where career discussions were focused on objectively evaluating options rather than giving directive advice or convincing people to stay. Remaining neutral doesn't mean being detached; rather, it's about recognizing that each person's circumstances are unique.

- **Encourage self-reflection through targeted questions:** When someone seeks advice, they're often at a career crossroads—contemplating a shift in roles, a major change in career focus or leaving a job or organization they've outgrown. Instead of prescribing a solution based on your own experiences, guide them through a series of reflective questions. What are their long-term goals? How satisfied are they in their current role? What risks are they willing to take, and what are their must-haves in terms of work-life balance? These questions help them clarify their own priorities and values, making it easier for them to identify the best path forward for their situation.

- **Help them visualize the implications of each option:** Guide the person in thinking through the tangible effect of their decision. What will their professional and personal life look like if they stay as is or make a change? What are the potential short and long-term consequences of each choice? These questions help them envision the implications of their decision for their life circumstances and long-term goals.
- **Empower them to own their decision:** The person seeking advice will ultimately have to live with the consequences of their decision. You will not. That's why it's crucial to enable them to take full ownership of their choice. While it might be tempting to offer strong, directive advice, doing so is presumptuous and could very well overlook the complexities of their life situation, be they financial concerns or work-life balance.

Offering impartial advice doesn't mean you lack concern for the person or aren't invested in the person's journey. It's quite the opposite. By being neutral in your guidance, you're providing a safe space in which they can explore their options without judgment or pressure. This shows that you care about their happiness and success and also that you respect their ability to make decisions for themselves.

Actively seek feedback for continuous improvement

Seeking and acting on feedback supports your continuous growth and development. Seeking out real-time feedback allows you to make small, immediate improvements that add up over time. More broadly, when the opportunity arises, embrace systematic 360-degree feedback for a comprehensive view of your strengths and areas for development.

> "Make feedback normal, not a performance review."
>
> — Ed Batista, executive coach

Ask for real-time feedback for ongoing improvement

Too many people wait for formal review periods or project conclusions to ask for feedback. To truly grow, it's best to incorporate real-time feedback into your routine. Real-time feedback allows you to address weaknesses and to correct course before any problem has a chance to establish itself, which puts you in a better position when it comes to an end-of-year review or other formal review occasion.

- **Seek specific, actionable insights:** When asking for real-time feedback, be precise in your requests to encourage clear and useful responses. A general question like "How did I do?" may not yield detailed feedback. Instead, target specific aspects of your performance with questions like "Was my presentation clear?" or "Did I give everyone enough time to share their thoughts?" This way, you're more likely to receive focused advice that you can act on immediately. For instance, if you're told that your meeting delivery was rushed, you can slow down and be more mindful in your next session. The clearer your question, the more actionable the feedback.

- **Use informal moments to gather feedback:** Some of the best feedback comes from informal settings, right after a meeting or presentation when the experience is fresh in everyone's mind. Take advantage of these spontaneous moments by asking, "Is there anything I could have done differently to get more client engagement?" Because these discussions aren't bound by the structure of a formal review, you're more likely to get honest, unfiltered responses. This can lead to candid insights that might not surface in more structured settings, providing immediate pointers you can incorporate right away.

- **Involve a range of colleagues:** Don't limit your feedback requests to your manager. While your manager can provide valuable high-level insights, your peers and direct reports can offer a ground-level view of how you perform day-to-day. These colleagues often notice details your manager might miss. For example, asking a team member for their input on your delegation style might reveal areas for adjustment that your manager wouldn't catch. Engaging a diverse set of voices provides a well-rounded perspective on your strengths and areas for improvement.

It's important to consider feedback carefully, but don't let a single comment steer you too far off course. Focus on identifying recurring themes in the feedback you receive. For example, if multiple people suggest you need to improve your time management, that's a clear area for improvement. By contrast, a one-off comment that contradicts other feedback may not warrant a change in behavior. Weigh the advice against your broader experiences to decide if it's worth acting on or not.

Embrace 360-degree feedback for your overall career arc

Truly honest feedback can be hard to come by. Direct reports may hesitate to provide candid upward feedback for fear of offending their boss. Peers, caught between competition and collaboration, often temper their critiques to maintain harmony. Even managers, while aiming to offer constructive criticism, might prioritize motivation over complete candor to avoid discouraging you. One way to counter this problem is with 360-degree feedback, a feedback approach that gathers anonymous input on an individual's performance from multiple sources, including peers, direct reports, supervisors and sometimes clients. With multiple perspectives on how they are perceived, recipients have better data from which to draw conclusions about areas in which they need to make improvements and where and how they are doing well. Because the feedback is anonymous, the responses are more likely to reflect genuine opinions. This type of feedback gives recipients a more fulsome view of how they're perceived across all levels of the organization, often revealing areas that would otherwise remain hidden:

- **Approach feedback with humility and an open mind:** Receiving feedback—especially when it's comprehensive and unfiltered—requires a mindset of humility. It's natural to feel defensive when faced with criticisms that don't align with your self-image—which 360-degree feedback often generates. However, the most valuable insights often come from the feedback that's hardest to hear. For example, you might have always prided yourself on your decisiveness, only to learn that colleagues see it as a tendency to make hasty decisions without seeking input. Knowing this allows you to change the way you make or communicate decisions, and such changes could lead to substantial improvement in how you perform and are perceived by others.

- **Act on the feedback to show you're listening:** Collecting 360-degree feedback is only the first step; what truly matters is how you respond. Soliciting feedback from a range of people and then doing nothing with it can damage your credibility. Colleagues who took the time to provide thoughtful input expect to see some degree of change. Identify the most common or insightful pieces of feedback and make a concrete plan to address them. For example, if multiple people mentioned that you tend to dominate meetings, make a conscious effort to listen more and invite others to contribute. Taking visible steps to improve based on the feedback shows that you value the input and are committed to becoming a better professional.

- **Acknowledge and thank those who provided feedback:** Thanking the people who took the time to give you feedback builds trust and fosters a culture of open communication. In addition to thanking them, share what you've learned from the feedback and outline the steps you're taking to grow. For instance, you could say, "Based on the input I received, I'm working on being more concise in meetings, so everyone has a chance to speak." By sharing this commitment, you demonstrate a willingness to make changes and encourage a culture of continuous feedback. Consider asking for follow-up feedback to gauge whether your efforts to improve have been noticed and are having the desired effect.

Use conversations to manage your career trajectory and celebrate accomplishments

Although I've warned in earlier sections about the dangers of seeking undue credit, it's right and proper to advocate for yourself as you work toward your career goals. Similarly, you should take the time to enjoy your successes—and you should encourage others to celebrate their own, as well.

Take charge of your career through self-advocacy

Managing your career successfully often comes down to understanding the difference between seeking credit and advocating for yourself. While seeking credit can come off as self-serving, self-advocacy is necessary activity to make your aspirations visible to those who can help you achieve them:

- **Communicate your goals clearly:** Whatever your aspirations—whether you're aiming for a promotion, a new project or a change in your role—make them known. Don't rely on your managers to guess your desired next career move or to automatically offer you growth opportunities just because you're doing a good job. In larger organizations, managers often have limited time to focus on each individual's career goals. A simple way to initiate this conversation might be during a performance review. You can say, "I'm looking to take on more leadership responsibilities, and I'd appreciate your guidance on how to get there."

- **Set clear expectations for your development:** You need to be specific in expressing your expectations about what should come next for you. If you believe that your high performance should lead to a promotion or new opportunities, be explicit about it but not aggressively so. For example, saying, "I'd like to understand how my current performance could lead to a more senior role in the next six months. What specific milestones should I be aiming for to make that happen?" both makes your expectations clear and shows that you are willing to take steps to achieve them. This approach opens the door for constructive dialogue about your growth path.

- **Ask for leadership capital:** Beyond expressing your goals, ask for support, or leadership capital, from your mentors or managers. This means requesting their advocacy in important conversations, their investment in your skill development and their influence in helping you access new opportunities. For instance, you might say, "I'd like your support when I make my case for that upcoming project lead role." You are asking them to actively champion your career progression.

- **Be mindful of timing and phrasing:** Knowing when and how to advocate for yourself is just as important as the message itself. Choose moments that are naturally geared towards career discussions, like planning sessions or performance reviews, rather than inserting your goals into unrelated conversations. Frame your remarks around the value you bring to the organization and your long-term aspirations rather than listing out your achievements. For example, you might say, "I see myself as adding value as a practice leader, as someone who can grow a new business, not just lead projects in our current business. I would like to see my role evolving to contribute more directly to new-business development. Can we talk about how I can position myself for those opportunities?"

- **Know what you don't want:** Self-advocacy includes being clear about the opportunities you don't want. Saying no is just as important as saying yes when a project or role doesn't align with your career goals. Politely declining an assignment that doesn't fit your long-term vision shows that you're thoughtful and deliberate about your career trajectory. You might say, "I appreciate being considered for this role, but my focus right now is on developing skills that align with my goal of moving into leadership. Can we explore other opportunities that would help me build toward that?"

Waiting passively for recognition or advancement is risky. Others are likely advocating for themselves, and if you don't do the same, you might get overlooked. It's not about being pushy but about making people aware of what you have to offer.

"If opportunity doesn't knock, build a door."

— Milton Berle, actor and comedian

Be proud of yourself and encourage others to congratulate themselves

When we see colleagues, friends or family members achieve something significant, it's natural to say, "I'm proud of you" or "I really admire what you've accomplished." We want to express admiration and share in their moment of success. But another powerful thing you can say is "You should/must be proud of yourself." This subtle shift in language encourages individuals to fully own and enjoy their accomplishments:

- **Encourage self-recognition:** Too often, people breeze past their accomplishments, focusing on the next task without pausing to acknowledge what they've done. Telling someone, "You should/must be proud of yourself," prompts them to reflect on their achievements and helps them take a moment to appreciate the hard work and dedication that led to their success. If a colleague delivers a stellar presentation, instead of just saying, "Great job," try saying, "You should be proud of how well you handled that presentation." This encourages a sense of personal pride.

- **Apply the practice to personal relationships:** This approach isn't limited to the workplace; it's equally effective in personal relationships. When guiding children, encouraging them to be proud of themselves fosters self-confidence and resilience. For example, instead of always telling your child, "I'm so proud of you," say, "You should be proud of yourself for working so hard on that project." This builds their self-esteem and teaches them to recognize and value their own efforts, beyond seeking external validation. (In this situation and the one above, you can and should still follow up with "I am proud of you.")

- **Practice self-recognition in your own life:** This mindset is something you should embrace for yourself, too. Take a moment to quietly congratulate yourself for even the smallest accomplishments. Whether it's meeting a deadline, mastering a new skill or handling a challenging situation, acknowledging your own successes keeps you motivated and will help you maintain a positive outlook, even on days when the routine feels monotonous or overwhelming.

Valuing your own efforts and encouraging others to do the same contributes to a culture of success and provides a stronger sense of self-worth for everyone.

Consciously choose your work-life balance

There's another sort of presence that's crucial to success and happiness in your career and your larger life: presence in your decisions. By this I mean being truly aware of the choices and trade-offs you're making as you advance your career. You're always making decisions—but you're not always aware of them. Take work-life balance. It's often a struggle to get right, and more often than not, we simply let work win out over life's other demands. It's an unconscious decision, not a conscious one, and it often leaves us tired, disconnected or resentful. For many of us, it takes a jarring realization or a well-timed intervention by a family member or colleague to finally, consciously, rethink our priorities.

We should aim to be open and explicit with ourselves and those around us about our needs and desires, and we should use conversations purposefully to be transparent about those needs and the implications for ourselves and others.

Be deliberate in your work-life decisions

Making explicit decisions about your work-life balance doesn't mean you'll eliminate difficult trade-offs, but it does mean you will be conscious and thoughtful about what you're choosing and why. Are you missing family dinners because of work demands? Are you sacrificing personal time for that next promotion? The point isn't to find the perfect solution but to be clear about what works best for you and to make those decisions with your eyes wide open:

- **Resist the default mode of operation:** In today's work culture, where hustle and overachievement are celebrated, it's easy to let work take over your life. The default mode is to stay busy, to do more and to push harder even as our personal lives quietly erode. Instead, be deliberate about your work-life balance. This requires you to resist this automatic mode of operation and consciously decide where your time and energy are best spent. It's about recognizing that while work can be rewarding, it shouldn't come at the cost of your well-being or relationships. Ask yourself what you're really getting in return for all those late nights and missed family moments. Is it worth the trade-off? And if it isn't, what are you going to do about it?

- **Communicate your decisions clearly:** Once you've made these decisions, communicate them openly with those who matter—your partner, your family, your boss. Setting clear boundaries helps you and sets the right expectations for others. For example, let your loved ones know if you're choosing to focus on your career for the next few years, or let your employer know if you're scaling back on extra work to make time for family. When everyone knows your priorities, there is less chance of a misunderstanding.

- **Be willing to revisit and adjust:** Work-life balance isn't a one-time decision. It's a series of decisions you'll need to make again and again as your circumstances change. What works for you now might not work six months or a year down the line, and that's okay. The goal is to stay intentional about your choices, revisiting them as needed and adjusting your priorities based on what's most important in each phase of your life. The most important thing is to own your decisions fully.

My personal wake-up call

My wake-up call came from a senior colleague during a period when I was still adjusting to life as a new father. He shared a story that had a lasting effect on me—one that shaped how I approach my own work-life balance decisions.

He recounted how he had unknowingly sacrificed valuable family time for the sake of his career.

He had a son and daughter, some seven or eight years apart, and when his daughter was born, his wife had told him, "You need to spend much more time with your daughter than you did with your son." It wasn't until that moment that he realized how much he had missed in his son's early years while he was chasing career success. By the time he tried to repair that bond, his son was already a teenager. Through hard work, my colleague did rebuild their relationship, and the result was rewarding, but the process was painful.

My colleague wasn't suggesting that we can rewrite the past—that's a fool's errand. Rather, he was saying that it's important to be fully conscious of the choices we make. He said that had he made those decisions with complete awareness, he still might have made the same choices, but at least he would have done so with an understanding of the consequences. This sense of ownership over his choices, he felt, would have been empowering rather than disheartening.

Inspired by his story, I decided to take a step back and look at my own situation. Within a few months, I made a significant career shift, moving to a role that offered me more time with my family, even if it meant a reduction in financial rewards, status and career options. This wasn't an easy choice by any means, but it was the right one for me. Every moment I now spend with my kids, I'm reminded of the importance of making intentional decisions about where I invest my time and energy.

> "Never get so busy making a living that you forget to make a life."
>
> — Dolly Parton, singer and actress

* * * * *

Feedback and career conversations are powerful tools for shaping your professional journey and supporting others on theirs. Through giving and receiving feedback, advocating for yourself and managing your work-life balance and role choices, you lay the groundwork for sustained growth and success. Next, in the book's conclusion, we'll reflect on the core principles covered in *Power in Presence* and how they come together to create a cohesive strategy for mastering professional conversations.

Conclusion

In concluding, we encourage you to embrace the art of being present in all your conversations to enhance and accelerate your professional career.

Cultivate the Art of Being Present

As we conclude our journey through the essential elements of effective business conversations, remember that mastering presence in communication is not a one-time achievement but an evolving process. This guide has provided you with foundational strategies, advanced techniques and insights into the importance of staying informed, broadening your horizons and being respectful and inclusive. You are prepared for a wide range of conversational scenarios, including meetings, informal conversations and career discussions.

The challenge now is to use these tools in your work life. Treat each conversation as an opportunity to inform, persuade and inspire those around you. Be mindful of your presence, listen actively and strive to understand the needs and perspectives of others. Embrace different personality and thinking styles and create a more inclusive dialogue that leads to deeper understanding and stronger relationships.

Think of this guide as your companion in the art of business conversations—one that encourages you to push beyond the familiar, experiment with new techniques and learn from every interaction. As you grow in your career, continue to refine your skills, remain open to feedback and be adaptable in your approach. Conversations are not just about exchanging words; they are about building connections, fostering trust and driving influence.

Above all, remember that your presence in any conversation has the power to shape outcomes, create opportunities and leave a lasting impact. So, keep refining your ability to connect with others, embrace the journey of continuous improvement and let your authentic voice leave a lasting impression in every professional interaction.

> "It's all about communication, people. It's all about communication."
>
> — Elizabeth Gilbert, journalist and author

Exercises for Sharper Conversatons

Exercises for Sharper Conversations

The following exercises will help you put the ideas in Power in Presence into practice. Each one focuses on a different dimension of effective business conversation—self-awareness, understanding nonverbal cues, meeting engagement and giving feedback. There is also an exercise for consolidating your skills.

You can do the exercises in any order. I recommend focusing on one exercise per month (though you'll be asked to keep practicing aspects of each exercise in the month that follows), giving yourself time to observe, test and reflect before moving on. Exercise 5, for consolidating your skills, will reinforce what you learn by helping you notice, week by week, how fully you bring attention and presence to each interaction.

These exercises are opportunities for reflection and experimentation. Use them to notice patterns, test new behaviors and strengthen the habits that make your conversations clearer, more effective and more authentic. If possible, invite a trusted colleague, mentor or manager to offer periodic feedback as outside perspectives can reveal progress and blind spots you might not see yourself.

Exercise 1: Recognize how your personality shapes your communication

Purpose: Reflect on how your personality profile and natural communication style shape your conversational strengths, limits and blind spots.

Step 1: Identify your conversational traits

Choose **three traits** that describe how you tend to communicate in professional settings. If you're unsure, review the list below and mark the ones that resonate most. Try to identify two traits that describe how you usually show up and one that represents a quality you're working to develop or manage.

Sample traits:

> Analytical | Empathetic | Direct | Reserved | Supportive | Curious | Structured | Cautious | Persuasive | Diplomatic | Reflective | Energetic | Spontaneous | Decisive | Detail oriented | Visionary | Measured | Harmonizing | Assertive | Analytical | Collaborative | Impatient | Perfectionistic | Self-critical | Overtalkative | Conflict averse | Skeptical | Risk averse | Easily distracted | Overanalytical

You can also draw traits from personality frameworks such as MBTI.

Step 2: Analyze the effect

For each trait, write 1–2 paragraphs reflecting on the following questions. Focus on specific behaviors and situations rather than general impressions:

- How does it show up in meetings or conversations (e.g., tone, pacing, listening, question style)?
- When does it help you communicate more clearly or build trust?
- When might it create friction—for example, by leading you to dominate airtime, hesitate to speak or overanalyze?
- What situational triggers bring out your less-helpful tendencies (e.g., stress, time pressure, senior audiences, conflict)?

Step 3: Consider feedback and perception

Expand your notes by reflecting on how others experience your communication style and what their reactions reveal about your self-awareness:

- What have colleagues, mentors or managers said (directly or indirectly) about your conversational presence or tone?
- Does their feedback confirm how you see yourself, or does it reveal blind spots?
- Whose reactions tend to surprise you most and why?

Step 4: Choose tactics to balance or stretch your style

Drawing on your reflections and lessons from this book, select **two practical tactics** you will experiment with during this month to refine your conversational style. For example:

- Pause three seconds after someone finishes speaking before responding.
- Invite one quieter participant per meeting to share a view.
- Replace qualifying phrases ("I might be wrong, but…") with declarative ones once per meeting.
- Limit yourself to one data point per contribution in strategy sessions to stay concise.

For both tactics you choose, answer the following questions:

- What skill or mindset are you strengthening?
- How will you remind yourself to apply it (e.g., a visual cue, written note, checklist or reminder from a peer)?
- What outcomes will tell you it's working?

Step 5: Reflect after the trial period

After a month of experimentation, add a short paragraph to your notes answering the following questions:

- What patterns did you notice when you consciously adjusted your style?
- Which tactic was easier to maintain?
- How did others respond or engage differently?
- What did you learn about the connection between self-awareness and conversational effectiveness?

Example insight: "Practice pausing before offering solutions so others have space to share their ideas. This will test whether my 'directive' trait limits collaboration."

Then take the next step:

- Choose **one tactic** to keep practicing and **one new tactic** to test next month.
- Capture your insights in a short summary (or in the presence journal in Exercise 5) so you can track your growth over time.

Exercise 2: Read the room and interpret nonverbal cues

Purpose: Strengthen your ability to observe, interpret and adjust to nonverbal cues—your own and others'—in meetings so you can respond with greater awareness and presence.

Step 1: Prepare to observe

Before you begin, familiarize yourself with common nonverbal cues. Review the table below or the full version in Part 3 to help you recognize what to watch for in upcoming meetings.

Type	Positive signs	Possible warning signs
Facial expressions	Relaxed, genuine smiles, steady gaze	Frown, clenched jaw, blank stare
Gestures	Open palms, nodding, inviting hand motions	Finger-pointing, crossed arms
Posture	Upright, leaning slightly forward	Slouching, leaning back, tense shoulders
Eye contact	Steady, natural	Avoiding or prolonged staring
Proxemics	Appropriate distance	Too close or too far
Mirroring	Subtle alignment	Exaggerated copying

Next, choose **three meetings** (in-person or virtual) you'll attend in the coming week. Before each meeting, note the following:

- Purpose of the meeting (e.g., status check, decision, coaching).
- Your role (chair, contributor, listener).
- One behavior you'll focus on most—for example, eye contact, posture or gestures.

Step 2: Observe and record

Immediately after each meeting, while impressions are fresh, complete one row in the observation grid you'll find at the end of this exercise. Keep notes brief—single words or short phrases are enough.

Example Observation Grid

Meeting	Positive cues you noticed (from others or yourself)	Cues that signaled tension, distraction or discomfort	What you tried or adjusted	What you'll try next time
Team check-in	Several people nodded and leaned forward while I spoke.	One participant crossed arms and stopped taking notes.	I paused and asked for their view directly.	Check in earlier next time to prevent disengagement.

Step 3: Analyze what you observed

After you've logged three meetings, write one to two paragraphs addressing the following questions:

- Which positive cues were most associated with openness or engagement?
- Which negative cues tended to signal distraction, tension or disengagement?
- Which of your own habits might unintentionally signal stress, impatience or dominance?
- How did your small adjustments affect others' openness or attention?

Step 4: Plan your next moves

Drawing on your observations, select **two nonverbal tactics** to practice in the remaining weeks of the month, such as:

- Relaxing facial muscles before speaking.
- Keeping both feet grounded and shoulders open when leading.
- Using hand gestures only when emphasizing key transitions.
- Pausing to make brief eye contact with two people before moving from one topic to the next.

For each tactic, note the following:

- When you'll apply it.
- How you'll remind yourself to do so.
- What outcome you'll look for (e.g., more questions from participants, fewer interruptions).

Step 5: Reflect on the learning

At the end of the month, add a short paragraph answering the following questions:

- What patterns did you start noticing automatically?

- Which adjustments improved engagement or trust?
- Which habits proved hardest to change—and why?
- What did this teach you about the relationship between physical composure, attention and influence?

Example insight: "When I consciously kept my arms uncrossed and leaned slightly forward while listening, others seemed more willing to jump in. The change felt small but shifted the energy of the discussion."

Then take it further:

- Choose **one cue or tactic** you'll continue practicing and **one new area** you'll observe next month (for instance, voice tone, discussed in Part 3's section on nonverbal communication).
- Record these insights in your presence journal (Exercise 5) so you can watch how nonverbal awareness strengthens your overall presence.

Observation Grid

Meeting	Positive cues you noticed (from others or yourself)	Cues that signaled tension, distraction or discomfort	What you tried or adjusted	What you'll try next time

Exercise 3: Lead meetings with focus and inclusion

Purpose: Identify and test small, deliberate behavioral changes that make meetings more productive, inclusive and impactful, whether you're the chair or a participant.

Step 1: Diagnose your current habits

Think about your recent meetings. In writing, answer the following questions:

- What do you already do consistently that works (e.g., start on time, summarize clearly)?
- What behaviors or dynamics frustrate you most (e.g., uneven airtime, meandering discussion)?
- What feedback—spoken or unspoken—have you received about how you run or contribute to meetings?

This short diagnostic helps you choose actions that matter.

Step 2: Choose three to five focus actions

Select a mix of process, people and presence actions. Use or adapt from the following list:

- **Process**: Clarify purpose, summarize midmeeting, end on time.
- **People**: Invite quieter voices, acknowledge contributions, redirect dominant talkers tactfully.
- **Presence**: Use purposeful pauses, maintain open posture, monitor tone.

Write each chosen action as a single sentence beginning with an active verb (e.g., "Invite at least one person who hasn't spoken to share a view before moving to the next topic").

Step 3: Plan your approach

For each action, answer the guiding questions in the meeting-habits planning worksheet at the end of this exercise.

Example Meeting-Habits Planning Worksheet

Action	Why it matters	When/where you'll test it	How you'll know it's working
Process: Summarize decisions halfway	Keeps alignment and prevents drift	Monthly project review	Fewer "rehash" discussions later
People: Invite quieter participant first	Builds inclusion and surfaces more ideas	Weekly team meeting	More balanced airtime; emergence of new perspectives
Presence: Use silence intentionally	Encourages reflection before response	One-on-one check-ins	Longer, more thoughtful answers; less interruption

Keep each entry concise—just enough to clarify your intent.

Step 4: Observe and adapt

Over the course of the month, ask yourself the following right after each meeting:

- Which behaviors felt natural? Which felt awkward?
- Did participants respond verbally or nonverbally?
- Did any change alter pace, tone or engagement?

A quick sentence or two after each meeting is enough to detect patterns.

Step 5: Reflect and extend

At month's end, write a short paragraph that answers the following questions:

- Which new behaviors produced the biggest improvement in energy, focus or outcomes?
- Which required significant effort and might need longer practice?
- How did these changes affect your confidence or credibility as a facilitator or participant?
- What behaviors did meeting chairs demonstrate that you would like to adopt?

Example insight: "Summarizing decisions halfway through kept the meeting on track and gave quieter colleagues confidence that their points had been heard. It also made the final wrap-up faster."

Then take the next steps:

- Select **one practice** to keep refining and **one new behavior** to test next month.
- Capture both in your presence journal (Exercise 5) so you can trace how meeting habits strengthen your overall presence.

Meeting-Habits Planning Worksheet

Action	Why it matters	When/where you'll test it	How you'll know it's working

Exercise 4: Plan and conduct effective feedback conversations

Purpose: Strengthen your ability to plan and conduct feedback or career-development conversations with clarity, empathy and balance and to learn from experiences over time.

Step 1: Plan your conversations

Choose **two or three people** you will meet with during the month. For each person, complete one row in the feedback planning worksheet at the end of the exercise. Keep your notes concise—phrases, not essays.

Example Feedback Planning Worksheet

Person (role)	Purpose and desired outcome	Core message or theme	Tone/mindset	Anticipated reactions and how you'll respond	Timing and key questions
Jordan (analyst)	Discuss missed deadlines → agree on time-management fix → rebuild trust	You're capable, but time management needs improvement	Calm, firm, supportive	Possible defensiveness → acknowledge effort first	Monday check-in (20 min); "What's making these handoffs hardest right now?"

In your conversation, use or adapt frameworks such as intent versus impact or "The effect on me" described in Part 5.

Step 2: Execute and observe

After each conversation, jot quick notes in the postconversation reflection worksheet at the end of the exercise. Keep entries short—just enough to capture the essence while it's fresh.

Example Postconversation Reflection Worksheet

Person	What went as planned	What surprised me	Next-time adjustment
Jordan	Stayed calm; they owned the issue quickly.	I overexplained early on.	Ask one question first, then pause.

Step 3: Reflect and integrate

Once you've completed the three conversations, write a short synthesis (less than a page) answering these questions:

- What patterns did you notice in how people responded?
- Which tone or framework created the most constructive dialogue?
- How did your own comfort or confidence change?
- What did you learn about giving feedback that could also help with how you receive and act on feedback from others?
- Which habits will you **continue**, **start** or **stop** using in future feedback or mentoring discussions?

Example insight: "When I began with a question rather than an evaluation, the conversation became collaborative. I learned that curiosity signals respect more effectively than reassurance."

Then take it further:

- Choose **one behavior** you'll refine and **one new behavior** you'll test in your next round of feedback.
- Record these insights in your presence journal (Exercise 5) to track how your feedback style evolves over time.

Feedback Planning Worksheet

Person (role)	Purpose and desired outcome	Core message or theme	Tone/ mindset	Anticipated reactions and how you'll respond	Timing and key questions

Postconversation Reflection Worksheet

Person	What went as planned	What surprised me	Next-time adjustment

Exercise 5: Monthly Presence Journal

Purpose: Consolidate what you've learned about how you show up in conversation, read the room, lead and participate in meetings and give feedback; build a steady habit of presence.

This journal helps you reinforce awareness and apply it across all your conversations so that you listen, focus and respond with intention.

Step 1: Set your intention

At the beginning of each month, write a short paragraph answering the following questions:

- What does being present in conversation mean to you now?
- Which habits, cues or tactics from Exercises 1–4 do you want to reinforce?
- What distracts or distances you most often (e.g., devices, multitasking, internal rehearsing, fatigue)?
- What benefits do you hope to see by practicing greater presence (e.g., better understanding, calmer tone, deeper rapport)?

Keep this paragraph at the top of your journal page as a personal compass for the month.

Step 2: Record your weekly reflections

Each week, capture one short reflection—just a few words or phrases in each column—on how present you felt in your conversations. Use the presence journal template at the end of this exercise (or adapt it in a notebook or digital document) and aim for four entries in total, one per week. As you write, note any small action or cue you practiced from earlier exercises—for example, pausing before replying, adjusting posture, inviting a quieter colleague or opening feedback with a question.

Example Presence Journal

Meeting	Moment I was most present or connected	Moment I disengaged or missed a cue	What I learned and what I will try next week	How I felt this week
1	Asked a quiet teammate for input; the discussion opened up quickly.	Glanced at phone midmeeting and lost my train of thought.	Presence dropped when I multitasked; engagement rose when I slowed the pace → Silence phone before meetings	More relaxed; felt genuine connection.

Tips:

- Keep each observation to a few words—just enough to capture the essence.
- Focus on awareness, not on attaining perfection; noticing itself is progress.
- If you miss a week, resume the following week; commitment matters more than completeness.

- As noted in the earlier exercises, you may wish to review one previous exercise each week as a lens for reflection.

Step 3: Spot your patterns

After four weeks, reread your entries and write a short paragraph reflecting on the following questions:

- When are you most naturally present? Small groups? One-on-ones? Virtual meetings? In person?
- What triggers distraction or tension now, compared with what you anticipated in Step 1?
- Which new habits improved your listening, composure or empathy?
- What signals from others (eye contact, nodding, leaning in) told you they felt your attention?
- Which cues or tactics from earlier exercises had the strongest effect?

Step 4: Integrate and carry forward

Close the month by summarizing, in two to three paragraphs, where you are now, taking into account the following questions:

- What does presence mean for you now?
- What are three habits you'll continue (e.g., silencing devices, pausing before speaking, paraphrasing key points)?
- What is one practice you'll drop that competes with presence (e.g., checking notes midconversation)?
- How will you remind yourself of your daily intention to stay present (sticky note, phone lock screen, pause briefly before each meeting)?

Revisit this summary before starting a new cycle. Your presence journal will be both a reflection record and a launchpad for continued growth.

Example insight: "I'm most present when I stop trying to anticipate my turn to speak. In week 3, I waited a few extra seconds after other people's answer, and the other person always added something deeper. Presence feels less like performance and more like calm attention."

Presence Journal Template

Meeting	Moment I was most present or connected	Moment I disengaged or missed a cue	What I learned and what I will try next week	How I felt this week

* * * * *

Bring it all together

Your power of presence grows through deliberate practice—first in noticing yourself, then by attuning to others and finally in guiding the flow of conversation with intention. Each exercise is a small experiment in awareness, empathy and clarity. Over time, these moments accumulate into instinct: you listen more deeply, respond more thoughtfully and engage with greater ease. Presence is not a single skill to master but a steady discipline of attention, one that turns everyday conversations into opportunities for genuine connection, influence and growth.

Index

A

abrasive colleagues, working with · 75, *see also* conflict, handling
active listening · 51–52, *see also* eye contact, use of
    avoid interrupting · 51
    eliminate distractions · 51
    focus on what's being said · 51
    paraphrase and summarize · 51
    reflect back emotions · 52
    use nonverbal cues · 51
agendas, use of · 24–25, *see also* chair, role of; meeting, managing a
    adjust, as needed · 25
    link meeting agenda to current news · 25
    link meeting agenda to venue · 25
    stay high level · 24–25
assistants, engaging executive
    avoid bypassing assistants · 17
    initial contact · 16
    respect the process · 16
    show appreciation · 17, 18
atypical, being
    be confident · 11
    beware of labels · 11
authentic, being · 7–9
    adapt over time · 9
    admit mistakes · 8
    be confident in your interests · 70
    challenges in being confident · 40–41
    communicate clearly · 6
    do not hold back · 8–9
    practice showing confidence · 41
    remain yourself · 8
    show interest in others · 6
    tailor your style · 6

B

body language, how to read · 44–46, *see also* eye contact, use of; interpersonal dynamics, managing; posture
    energy shifts · 45
    facial expressions · 44, 45
    gestures · 45
    group dynamics · 44–45
    posture and position · 41, 44, 45
    validate observations · 45

C

career discussions · 84–87, *see also* conversations and meetings, types of
    get support · 85
    offer impartial advice · 81–82
    self-advocacy · 84–85
    set clear expectations · 84, 85
    work-life balance · 86–87
chair, role of · *see also* agendas, use of; meeting, concluding, a; meeting, managing a; mind maps, use of; prepared or planted questions, use of; question-and-answer segment, managing a; time management
    adapt agenda, if needed · 25, 27
    avoid being too participative · 27–28
    balance speaking time · 28–29
    steer meeting · 27
Chatham House Rule · 24
    meaning · 24
    modified version · 24
    usage · 24
clichés · *see* plain English, use of
closed-ended questions, types of · 49, *see also* open-ended questions, types of
    dichotomous · 49
    fact-based · 49
    general yes/no · 49
    leading yes/no · 49
    multiple-choice · 49
    scale · 49
compliments, be careful offering · 73–74
conflict, handling · 62–66, *see also* abrasive colleagues, working with; politics and religion, avoid
    decide on next steps · 66
    encourage openness · 64
    find common ground · 65
    follow up · 65
    know when to agree to disagree · 66
    know when to escalate issues · 66
    maintain neutrality · 64
    propose solutions · 64
    rebuild conversation from point of alignment · 65
    reframe the conflict · 64
    seek compromise, if possible · 64–65
conflicts, scheduling · *see* meetings, scheduling
conversation, engaging in · *see also* career discussions; conversation, revive a dying; data, relatable; interpersonal dynamics, managing; plain English, use of; politics and religion, avoid; stay informed, how to
    avoid filler sounds · 57
    communicate clearly · 6
    encourage collaboration · 7
    engage others early on · 50–51
    focus on themes · 7
    show genuine interest in others · 6

conversation, revive a dying · 53
conversations and meetings, types of · *see also* career discussions
    career and performance discussions · 6
    feedback conversations · 6
    formal meetings · 5
    forums and conferences · 15
    informal · 5
    large meetings · 5–6, 15
    medium-sized meetings · 15
    one-on-ones · 15
    remote and virtual conversations · 6
    small meetings · 5, 15
corporate jargon · *see* plain English, use of
credit, giving and seeking · 46–47
    avoid credit seeking · 46
    be specific when offering credit · 46–47
    offer credit in front of senior colleagues and clients · 47

D

data, relatable
    emphasize effect · 59
    humanize numbers · 59
    simplify fractions · 59
    use familiar comparisons · 59
dress code
    official dress code · 39
    unofficial dress code · 39
    use judgment · 39–40

E

early-morning meetings · *see* meeting, scheduling
eye contact, use of · *see also* active listening; body language, how to read
    element of body language · 46
    importance of · 43, 46
    in large audiences · 44
    practice · 44
    when listening · 44
    when speaking · 43

F

facial expressions · *see* body language, how to read
feedback conversations · *see* conversations and meetings, types of
feedback, getting · 82–84
    360-degree feedback · 83–84
    act on feedback · 83–84
    real-time feedback · 82–83
    thank feedback giver · 84
feedback, giving · 79–81
    be constructive · 79, 80
    be private · 80
    impact and intent · 80–81
    legitimate feedback giver · 79–80
    offer practical alternatives · 79, 80
    "the effective on me" technique · 80
follow up, how to · *see also* virtual meeting, managing a
    be timely · 35
    highlight contributions · 35
    role in relationship building · 6
    show appreciation · 35
    summarize discussions · 35
foreign-origin terms · *see* plain English, use of
formal meetings · *see* conversations and meetings, types of

G

group dynamics · *see* body language, how to read

H

humor, use of · 47
    be aware of context and cultural matters · 47
    benefits of · 47
    be open · 47
    use to revive conversation · 53
hyperbole · *see* overstating and overqualifying, avoid

I

inclusive, being · *see also* plain English, use of
    accommodate real-time and reflective thinkers · 52
    avoid ableist language · 73
    avoid being artificially inclusive · 29
    be aware of gender dynamics when offering clarifying comments · 61–62
    be mindful of your idioms and metaphors · 72
    bring in junior colleagues · 29
    bring in known views · 29
    gender-neutral language · 72–73
    seating arrangement · 28–29
    use of preferred pronouns · 73
informal meetings · *see* conversations and meetings, types of
interpersonal dynamics, managing · 27–31, 39–47, *see also* body language, how to read
interruptions
    how to handle · 30
    how to handle in virtual meetings · 34
    know how to interrupt · 29–30
introductions
    allow individuals to introduce themselves · 23–24
    avoid embellishments · 9
    be concise · 23, 40
    junior colleagues · 23–24, 40
    know key milestones/transitions · 9
    know your backstory · 9

senior colleagues · 40
tailor to situation · 9

J

jargon · *see* plain English, use of

K

knowledge, broadening one's · 70–72
    ask clarifying questions · 71
    develop visual frameworks · 72
    learn from what you hear · 71
    seek out new roles · 71–72

L

language, clear · *see* plain English, use of
large-group meetings · *see* conversations and meetings, types of
late-night meetings · *see* meetings, scheduling
leave-behind materials · *see* materials, meeting
LinkedIn, use of · *see* meetings, preparing for

M

major problem, addressing a
    need to raise · 63
    offer solutions · 63
    prepare for resistance · 64
    take responsibility for outcomes · 64
materials, meeting
    avoid using unnecessarily · 20–21
    considerations on necessity · 20–21
    pre-prepared materials · 21
    purpose-developed materials · 21
    when to send · 21
meeting, concluding a · *see also* mind maps, use of
    cover next steps · 32
    outline achievements · 32
    stay focused on objectives · 31–32
meeting, managing a · *see also* agendas, use of; chair, role of; meeting, concluding, a; prepared or planted questions, use of; silence, use of; time management
    avoid someone taking control · 28
    determine and maintain right level of discussion · 26
    end on time · 33
    know how to interrupt · 29–30
    stay outcome oriented · 7
    take decisions · 7
meeting, recapping a · *see* mind maps, use of
meeting, requesting a
    avoid artificial connections · 16
    craft a hook · 16
    establish a connection · 16
    leave a voicemail · 16
    with known person · 15–16
meetings, preparing for · 19–22, *see also* materials, meeting
    avoid overpreparing · 19
    coach junior colleagues · 21–22
    complex meetings · 19
    preparation by email · 19
    preparatory calls · 19
    researching participants · 19–20
meetings, scheduling · 15–18
    avoid early-morning or late-night calls · 18
    avoid late calls on Friday · 18
    be mindful of time zones and locations · 17
    observe out-of-office markers · 17
    respect weekends · 18
    review calendars · 17
    use available calendar tools · 17
meetings, types of · *see* conversations and meetings, types of
metaphors · *see* plain English, use of
mind maps, use of · 32–33
    document topics · 32–33
    recap meeting · 33
Myers-Briggs Type Indicator · *see* personality assessments

N

names, use of
    pronunciation · 42
    spelling · 42
    use during conversations · 42–43
next steps · *see* meeting, concluding a
notetaking
    document decisions · 32
    how to take notes when leading a discussion · 54
    track agreed-upon actions · 32

O

open-ended questions, types of · 48–50, *see also* closed-ended questions, types of
    clarification · 50
    comparative · 50
    explanatory · 50
    opinion solicitation · 50
    probing · 50
    reflective · 50
overstating and overqualifying, avoid
    avoid hyperbole · 56
    avoid preambles and qualifying statements · 56
    avoid weakening superlatives · 56
    eliminate superfluous modifiers · 56

P

performance discussions · *see* conversations and meetings, types of
personality assessments · 10
    coping strategies · 10
    limitations · 10
    uses · 10
plain English, use of · 54–57, *see also* overstating and overqualifying, avoid
    avoid clichés · 55
    avoid corporate jargon · 55
    avoid foreign-origin terms · 55
    avoid sporting metaphors · 55
    balance use of lingo · 56–57
    benefits of · 54–55
    use simple verbs · 55
planted questions · *see* prepared or planted questions, use of
politics and religion, avoid · 62–63
    geopolitics versus politics · 63
    redirect discussion · 63
    show restraint · 63
posture · *see also* body language, how to read
posture, importance of · 41–42
preambles · *see* overstating and overqualifying, avoid
prepared or planted questions, use of · 31
pre-prepared materials · *see* materials, meeting
punctual, being · *see also* time management
    arrive on time · 23
    catch up · 23
    manage your schedule · 23
purpose-developed materials · *see* materials, meeting

Q

qualifying statements · *see* overstating and overqualifying, avoid
question-and-answer segment, managing a · 26–27, *see also* chair, role of
questions, use of · 48–51, *see also* active listening; closed-ended questions, types of; opened-ended questions, use of; prepared or planted questions, use of
    avoid prefacing · 48
    closed-ended questions · 49
    open-ended questions · 48, 50
    open up dialogue · 48–49

R

recognition
    avoid credit seeking · 46
    recognizing others · 18, 46–47
    self-recognition · 85
relationship building
    be patient in discussions · 43
    learn personal details · 43
    manage personal information carefully · 43
    use of questions · 43
religion · *see* politics and religion, avoid
remote meetings · *see* virtual meeting, managing a

S

self-aware, being
    avoid accentuating hierarchy · 60–61
    avoid clarifying others' remarks · 61–62
    avoid dominating conversation · 61
    use of *we* instead of *I* · 60
sharp-elbowed colleagues · *see* abrasive colleagues, working with
silence, use of · 31
    count in your head · 31
    use · 31
small group meetings · *see* conversations and meetings, types of
small talk · *see* stay informed, how to
sporting metaphors, avoid · 55
sports as a topic of conversation · 8, 69–70
stay informed, how to · 69–70
    news and business · 69–70
    pop culture · 70
storytelling
    build a library of stories · 58
    components of a good story · 58
    practice · 58
    respect others' stories · 52–53
    use of · 57–59
superfluous modifiers · *see* overstating and overqualifying, avoid
superlatives · *see* overstating and overqualifying, avoid
swear words, use of · 74–75

T

Teams meetings · *see* virtual meetings, managing a
time management · *see also* chair, role of
    manage time actively · 26
    use of clock or watch for timing · 26

V

virtual meeting, managing a · 34, *see also* agendas, use of; chair, role of; interruptions; time management
    encourage participation · 34
    manage audio and interruptions · 34
    need for follow up · 34
    observe body language · 34
    stay focused · 34
    use an agenda · 34

use technology features · 34

W

weekend meetings · *see* meetings, scheduling
work-life balance · *see* career discussions

Z

Zoom meetings · *see* virtual meeting, managing a

About the Author

With over three decades of experience, Mark Watson excels in financial services, governance and risk management. His career spans influential roles working with Britain's Conservative Party, the Adam Smith Institute, McKinsey & Company, Moody's, Tapestry Networks and EY.

Mark has been writing throughout his career, whether responding to proposed legislation, producing leading industry surveys or creating action-oriented reports for investors, board directors and senior executives. He has covered a wide array of topics, including governance, risk management, digital transformation and many more.

Mark has written and edited millions of words, created thousands of data-rich charts, presented at hundreds of events and conversed with thousands of leaders. He has drawn on these experiences in writing *Power in Presence*. He has authored a sister book, *Power in Precision*, on effective business writing.

He lives in Concord, Massachusetts—a fitting home for a UK/US dual national, given its historical significance as the birthplace of the American Revolution.

Acknowledgements

Conversation matters. I realized this at an early age. But conversing well is hard. As a child, I had a bit of a stutter, often because I rushed to enter a discussion without thinking things through or was vying to get a word in with one or more of my argumentative family. Despite projecting confidence, I was naturally introverted.

Early in my career, I knew I wanted to engage with influential people—older, wiser, more experienced professionals—so I had to find my inner confidence. I couldn't sit and wait for self-assurance to magically appear, nor could I afford to let my youth or inexperience hold me back. At the time, I still stuttered occasionally and lacked the polish that comes with experience, but I knew one thing: if I showed up to important meetings projecting uncertainty, I'd never be taken seriously. Fortunately, I had the opportunity to engage with many high-powered individuals—including three former prime ministers, more than 10 billionaires, over 350 CEOs and thousands of directors and executives. These people weren't obligated to meet with me; they chose to. I told myself that if they were willing to sit across from me, they respected me enough to hear what I had to say and valued the discussion. That shift in mindset became the foundation of my confidence.

One pivotal moment in my communication journey came when I received some stinging feedback. In 2003, fresh into my job in Parliament after months of networking and hard work, an executive assistant to a Member of Parliament (MP) pulled me aside and said, "The [MP] has noticed you don't pronounce your T's." My first reaction was to take offense—it felt like a criticism of my accent, something deeply personal to me. But after some reflection, I realized that the feedback wasn't an attack but a crucial insight into a barrier that could limit my growth in a place where clear communication was essential. I decided to adapt. Over time, I consciously worked at modifying my speech. That piece of feedback, though difficult to hear, helped me reach my full potential in ways I never expected.

I've met and learned from some truly exemplary conversationalists. During my time in politics, I witnessed the power of oration firsthand. The best politicians and policy influencers have a remarkable ability to communicate complex issues in simple, memorable ways. I had the privilege of working with effective communicators like Bernard Jenkin MP and Madsen Pirie, Adam Smith Institute founder. I admired the engaging style of people like Ann Robinson, a public policy leader. In the business world, conversations with executives like the former Bear Stearns CEO Jimmy Cayne and investors like the billionaire Sam Zell deepened my appreciation for storytelling that conveys a message with emotional resonance. Directors such as Laban Jackson and Anton van Rossum showed me that authenticity—being true to yourself—truly matters. Discussions with leaders like Jamie Dimon, JPMorgan Chase CEO, and James Gorman, chairman emeritus of Morgan Stanley, underscored the powerful effect of exuding confidence paired with intellect. Observing figures like Kristalina Georgieva, managing director of the International Monetary Fund, and Debra Perry, former Moody's senior executive, helped me understand the importance of reading the room and fostering inclusivity in every interaction. I appreciate all these free lessons on how to engage and inspire others in conversation.

Above all, I'm profoundly grateful for my family: my wife Kathryn and our wonderful children, Soren, Aurora and Caden. They make life worth living, and without question, my favorite conversations are with them. They are smart, engaging, witty and warm—and they rarely let me win an argument. Kathryn deserves special thanks. She has let me debate for almost 30 years, only occasionally closing me down when I'm on a roll (typically when I've argued myself into a corner). She also gave me the time and support to write *Power in Presence* and its sister *Power In* books on business writing, data visualization and presentations. Without Kathryn's patience and love, I'd have stalled in my twenties.

Praise for *Power in Precision: A Guide to Effective Business Writing*

"The world needs better writers. We all spend much of our time in informal exchanges where punctuation is optional, spelling has become phonetic, phrases are reduced to four letters (all CAPS), and emojis tell the story. In some linguistic sense, it is fascinating. But formal writing hasn't gone away. *Power in Precision* should be compulsory reading for college students and young professionals who want career success and lasting impact in any field."

— Jennifer Banner, Corporate Board Director, Industry Research Fellow MIT Center for Information Systems Research, and Former Corporate Executive.

"Overall *Power in Precision* is very well done. Aligning what you think with what you say and what you write so that others understand you precisely and exactly is an art and a science that few learn and even fewer teach. This book guides the way."

— Nicholas Donofrio, IBM Fellow Emeritus, former IBM Executive Vice President, Innovation and Technology, and Author, *If Nothing Changes, Nothing Changes*.

"Mark Watson's *Power in Precision* offers business economists and new writers a primer and a style guide on how to write more clearly and directly. We all need this as we draft memos for our CEOs, or prepare policymakers for testimony, or present to large general audiences. Watson's call for better writing is on target. Much we read today can be imprecise, turgid, and riddled with jargon or clichés. If you want to reach your audience by improving your writing skills, this book is for you."

— Stuart Mackintosh, International Economist, former Group of Thirty Executive Director, and Author, *Climate Crisis Economics* and *The Redesign of the Global Financial Architecture*.